And When The Bough Broke

A mother's personal account of her family's battle to survive terrifying grief and discover life after the tragic loss of her youngest son, Charlie.

Elise Normile

Dedication

Jay, I am grateful for your tireless devotion and your genuine love for us all. You remain my everything, always, and forever. EnJ

Gaela, you gifted me with the role of mother. You have delighted me every day since we first met. I remember crying when you were born because I knew I would have to share you with others and the time I had with only you would never again be as constant as the pregnancy.

My sweet baby James, your acts of love for me have been epic and remarkable since you were a child. The letters you've written me, the flowers you've brought me, the ice water, dinners, aspirin, gentle assistance, compliments.... You are a good and gentle spirit. May you always know how much I love you. Of all of the children, I only shed tears for your first day of kindergarten. Somehow the separation seemed the most profound and difficult.

Jack Jack, you are the piece that fits my puzzle. My rough and tumble zest for life and lover of fun times. You are my only child who shares my book choices and desire to gain new experiences. You love to be picked, participate, volunteer, dance, sing, paint.... You have always lived a life that no one could regret, for no matter how limited the days, you live each one to the fullest. Why not and well done... you inspire me.

Lola, my silly little muffin. My baby princess. My strawbaby. Oh, Lola... I am so sorry for your loss. Your dedication and devotion to Charlie's memory is so touching. Wearing so many different items of his, talking of or him or to him each day, laughing about old memories and asking me, "Do you remember THAT?!"... Oh, Lola, you are the dearest, youngest widow the world may ever know... May Charlie remain by your side to witness your joyful and lonely moments... and may you know that he is there.

Charlie.. My Char baby...Oh Charlie, this is just so awful. Mommy is so sad without you. Doesn't God want you to comfort me more often than you do? Char, I hate to be pushy...but, it is really just so difficult without you. You were still at the utter devotion, kissy, bright eyed adoration of me... and the severing of my responsibilities to you, the end of the kisses and embraces, the sleepy head leaning back against my shoulder... My Charlie-less life has proved staggering. Char Char, momma loves you... I always did. I always will. I will work hard to make you proud and to remain the happy heart you knew so that when I come to you, you'll know me immediately and run to me once again.

Our love for one another is simply remarkable. May my love and devotion speak my thanks.

On Saturday, May 19th, our two and half year old son slipped unknowingly into our backyard swimming pool. After being discovered by his 9 year old brother, he began a 6 day fight for life in the Pediatric Intensive Care Unit. Our youngest child, Charlie passed away, Friday, May 26th leaving his 15 year old brother, James, 16 year old sister, Gaela, and 9 year old brother, Jack to begin an involuntary battle with grief and sadness. Fortunately, Charlie's twin, Lola, seems oblivious to the tragedy. My husband and I attempt to survive and lead our family out of these dark days... This is our story...

"Hi, Chubby."   <jack>

"Hi Charlie"   <gaela>

"Why don't you come and play with us? We got.. Me and Lola and Gaela have a purple lollipop for you."

"Chubby, I hope you, I hope you come awake and come wrestle with me…." <james>

"Hey Chubby… I hope you wake up soon… You want ice cream? It's me Jack Jack"

"and Gaela and Lola"

"Hi chubby. What are you doing? Wanna play soccer? Wanna wrestle? What are you doing, Chubby? Wake Up It's me, James. Wanna lollipop? Me and Lola have a purple lollipop"_

"Hi Chullie.   Hi Chullie.   Hi Chullie.   Hi CHULLIE…….   Mom-meeeee. I need help finding Chullie in there_"_ (lola)

_"HI__ It's me, MOMMY_ I looovve you_ Wanna come play? Want me to pick you up? Ok_ I'll pick you up. What do you want to play?"_

It's me… Gaela.   What are you doing?   Wanna come play? Wanna play with us?"

Pieces of the audio recordings made by Charlie's siblings that his parents played against his ear, over and over again, to rouse him from his coma. No response was ever noted or recorded.

Life Takes a Turn Towards Hell

The morning May sun shined brightly into the bedroom and I awoke with a start. "School day or weekend? School day or weekend?", I thought with a panic. As a school teacher, the failure of an alarm clock was an ever present fear. Think. Think. Today is First Communion for second grade., Yes, today at 5 pm, many of my second graders would make their First Communion sooooo.... Weekend it is.

Rather than covering my head and attempting to sneak more sleep, I bounded from bed. Weekends meant I had far more time to enjoy my treasures- my five dear children. Including the lovely, affectionate duo of Lola and Charlie. My 2 ½ year old twins were unlimited in their maternal love which made it difficult to leave them for school or store. But, today, yes, today was the weekend and in just 4 short days, the entire summer would be ours to love and enjoy together... little did I know then that one of our lives would end completely and all of our lives would end what they were in just five more short hours.

As I entered the kitchen, I saw a note from my 16 year old daughter, Gaela, letting me know she had left to run in a 5k neighborhood fundraiser for MS. I was inspired to support her. I quickly hugged and twirled Charlie and Lola, fed them breakfast, and got them changed. In mere moments, they were zippered into a bike seat carrier and I was pumping towards the race to support my dear sweet, Gaela.

As we approached the race, I was winded and decided to stop and cheer from the sidelines rather than riding with the runners for support. I unzipped the carrier and Charlie, with sunglasses on upside down and Lola, with wrong footed sandals shouted, "Hi" and "hello" to every runner that passed.

Later that day, I left my twins with a kiss. It was my final kiss for one of them as I went to buy groceries for a special family barbeque. In less than two hours, a wonderfully close happy family built with love over the last 17 years would be traumatically and permanently changed.

The entire morning was perfect. The race, buying plants with Charlie for our garden, and planning a family picnic were all perfect. The day was too perfect, my nine year old son, Jack would later observe.

I Miss You, Charlie
Jack, Age, 9

The day Charlie died was terrible. I felt sick to my stomach. I couldn't stop thinking about him and couldn't stop crying. It was the worst day of my life seeing him there limp, face down, pale...it all just scarred me. Right now, life is terrible without him. I remember now more than ever things he always said, like "dee-leecious" and shaking his head side to side. As I'm writing with a hurt stomach, I will just cry. I don't want to think about him or it will make me cry some more. To write I need my mind and all that's in my mind is how much I miss Charlie and the way I saw him limp, face down, and pale. Charlie was my best and one of two closest friends....Charlie and Lola. Lola was my second friend and she was the loving one. Charlie was the fighting one. Whenever Charlie tried to beat me up, Lola would hug me and give me a kiss where Charlie had either bit or scratched me.

Mom's Journal

The Final Day of Hell... We prepare to leave

5.26.2011   3:30 pm

We stood outside the Pediatric Intensive Care Unit (PICU) drained of emotion. Not sad or angry, but rather joyless and tired. Empty. We were the hollow people. We lifted the PICU phone for the final time to gain entry.

"This is Charlie's Mom and Dad"

Charlie was dead and wasn't coming home, but we were determined that everything that was with him **would** be coming home.

"This is Charlie's Mom and Dad"…. The present tense for the last time. He is active in this sentence, we are his parents and he is present tense. We were calm, matter of fact. It was normal. Of course we were his parents and everyone on staff recognized us that way. I should have grabbed the pink post it note from our hospital door. The one that said, "Charlie's Parents" in a casual cursive "of course you are" manner.

It wasn't posted on Charlie's hospital door, but ours. The one they gave us to sleep in. Dull, grey paint. Small twin beds. No television. Jay said the beds were like sleeping on waxed paper or a bag of chips. The crunch of plastic. We didn't want to be in there very much anyway, but the room made it easier… an architectural shoehorn lifting us right back to Charlie's side.

Have you lost something or someone you loved? What details do you recall from the first moments?

Day one of a life I never wanted.

Today has been busy...We have been on the road travelling to Gaela's soccer tournament. It is a sunny, warm Friday of Memorial Day Weekend...people sit on Chick's Beach as we begin our journey. How can they sit there? The sun just makes me feel gray and sickly. Jay comments on how blue the waters of the Chesapeake Bay are...I stay silent...I will not participate. Water. He should know better. "The water is so pretty, "he continues, and Gaela leans forward to agree. I try to be angry at his normal tone...does he feel normal? I won't be mad if he does...I am just curious. Is he "Mr. Vacationing Dad" already? I am slightly impressed.

"Honey, don't look at the water until you put on my sunglasses," he urges as he hands me his pair. Jay always marvels at the beauty of colors a good pair of Costas can bring... I put the glasses on...To refuse would require words...words require thought...thought requires a mind. And well, mine has been a bit undependable to say the least... on the fritz...on the blink... Like one of those old antenna televisions that seemed to only operate with a bang of the hand... Yes, a hard bang with the flat palm of the hand. A bang on the top or a bang to the side of the tv. It didn't matter. So my mind's on the blink as they say... Could it possibly just need a bang of the hand?

I find myself silently putting the glasses on to look at water I don't want to look at...in a life I don't want to live...And, the waters **are** bluer...and I feel nothing... I looked at the water and I didn't feel anything. Imagine that....no grief. No images of Charlie. No sadness. I return the glasses to Jay and stare ahead...I have no more thoughts. Thoughts require a mind. And well, mine is on the fritz.

Do you recall moments where your thoughts were fuzzy? What do you remember about those moments?

An hour earlier....On the way out of town.

Gaela and I run into Walgreens to pick up a prescription, toothpaste, and road trip snacks. The prescription needs a photo id and so Gaela runs to the car to retrieve mine. I browse....tired and empty...A hollow person with an uncooperative mind. We return to the line and wait impatiently for the slow customers and the snail paced clerk.

I stare at the back of the customer's head in front of me. "Do you know what happened?" I silently ask of her. "Do you even know who I am?" I stare at the sunburned face of the gentleman on the cell phone. Can he tell? My back aches and I shift my weight. I sigh from the pain and put my basket on the counter. "Say anything," I think. I dare any of them to say anything to me. I am ready. "My back hurts," I'll explain, "And my son died yesterday." They will retreat in horror. For, I am one of them...The Hollow People...right here standing before them.

Hollow People hold a badge of power. A permission to do anything...an involuntary suspension of insecurities...other people's opinions of you fail to matter. You're a veteran of the Death Wars...You've been to Hell and survived. Damaged, yes certainly damaged, but standing...and standing here among you. There is some satisfaction with this power we the Hollow People hold. But, it comes at a steep price. And isn't easy to obtain...This badge of power is death's trade...And you'll discover it where your loved one used to be... an acceptance to an unwilling army of isolated souls.

The road trip continues on.... Silence... sadness... small town after small town. I became aware that Jay wants to ask me something. "Why don't you just ask what you're thinking?" I demand of him. "I'm afraid of upsetting you", he admits. I insist he continue and he asks if I want to know if the doctors determined if Charlie has organs that can be gifted to others.... "Absolutely", I say in a light, breezy way and I mean it. I'm strangely excited about the topic. "I want to know everything about my son" I explain with pride... I look at the window again silently surprised by this joyous adrenaline.... It occurs to me that it was simply nice to hear of Charlie in the present tense still. That he is still doing things... "Did I tell you Charlie's class went to the museum today?" I picture sharing with a neighbor. "Did I tell you Charlie's kidney is off to Kansas" ... That's a lovely place, isn't it?

Will these be the final living statements about my boy? The life gifts he provided to unknown families of the dying? I fail to be lifted. It doesn't seem to heal.... Then I remember the 6 day battle I waged against death. Night and day, day and night... My husband and I sat walked and prayed together nearly 20 hours a day. We became one soul for a time as we took turns praying, then holding Charlie's hand, and calling out to rouse him. One morning when I walked to the vending machine, I stopped to watch people passing and to have silence for a time. Jay called hysterically looking for me and I rushed back to find him leaning against a wall...stooped and sobbing. His tremendous pain had forced him from Charlie's side and he wailed in grief. Charlie's donations of life will certainly comfort us in time.

No parent can appreciate the profound value of life until they have had it threatened to such a degree that they must wait painfully on the national donor list. I remember as a child going to amusement parks and there was always a lengthy line for that season's newest roller coaster. The line to ride might require over 2 hours of your patience. As the day winds down, you might wonder if you'll get to the start of the line and ride the coaster before the park closes... People with failing organs stand on a lengthy line for life, hoping with desperation that the stupid line moves faster before death closes the whole thing down. Imagine the panic and patience that must co-exist in these poor lives.

Well, since writing this entry, I have learned that a lovely dying 22 month old daughter and child, has won Charlie's heart.... a little South Carolina southern belle... She remains anonymous and the family has not yet reached out to us. But she is thriving and alive. The mere basic information we have is enough to praise Jesus that He allowed our little boy to live a of significance to others and save a young child's life. We possibly know more than anyone what a gift that knock on the hospital door would mean to terrified parents.... it is a knock that saves...I wish we could have heard it on our hospital door.... I'd much rather be running him to the park than remembering all I can of him. Run, jump, and dance in the sunshine little girl.... its your silly, new heart you have... and live your life towards God, remembering that most of your heart's body is already with Him.

Have you been hollow? Where were you when you felt surprise at the normal world that moved around your private pain?

Day 1: Or is it Day 2? (2:30am)

Earlier today, when packing for the trip, I found something. I found that I was totally fearless in this new life. Not fearless in the complimentary (Did you hear my mom walks a tightrope?) kind of way. Literally, I am fearless. (i.e. afraid of nothing.) For isn't the greatest fear that of death? And how could I be afraid of death now? Ha.... Death means **nothing** to me now. Death for me will bring the reunion. hmmm. .. So....reaalllly... I suppose death means *everything* to me now.

Don't bother envying the fearlessness of the hollow. We lie. We have one fear that is SO great and so punishing that we suffer it silently... quite literally, refusing to even speak this fear into existence. I refer to the fear of forgetting.... everything and anything about him.

Day 2 of A Life I Never Wanted

4:15am… The hotel is dark and moist…The air condition chugs, but fails to cool the warm air. My family snores gently as I sit in the dark and think. My mind is empty… I consider curiously how life became a series of tags, names, and records. Everything now has a label. The first road trip without Charlie. Charlie has never been on this highway. Charlie's books. The first night without him. The first time I buy small pink flip flops without buying a pair of blue also…

I consider how I'd used the power of the hollow people earlier in the day. Jay had been stopped for speeding, 67 in a 55, on the back roads of Route 13. No one has ever escaped a ticket from these tireless, ticketing troopers… He approaches the car and Jay begins to talk to him and I burst into tears and say "My son died yesterday… This little girl's twin." "Ma'am" he cautions me loudly. He puts his hand up and tells me to stop. He continues to talk to my husband and I begin again and look him in the eyes. " I can prove he died", I sob with pain. He lifts his arm again and backs up quickly. "That's enough_" he barks and retreats to the squad car coldly. I am stunned at his response. No warmth. No understanding. We'll be ticketed for sure. What robotic soulless fiber is this man made of? When he returns, though, he has only issued us a warning… a warning_ Now I know what I saw in him earlier. The retreating, the barking, the quick defensive lift of his arms…

It was fear. I was hollow. I had death near me. Maybe still on me. Hadn't I offered proof? I thanked the officer and told him he should call his mother and tell her what a good thing he'd done for a mother who's son had died…. He briefly glanced in my direction and looked away again. The tired, sunken cheeks. The lifeless eyes. The fearless shrug I threw around about death. I was a warrior and he was unmatched… My final demand had mentioned his mother and the trooper was breathless and tripping to escape.

The car ride resumes. I stare ahead. Silent again. Jay talks on about cruise control and using care with speed. I am unable to respond. I stare out the window. No one bothers to say we are lucky. We are not lucky. I retrieve the warning slip the trooper had issued from a garbage bag in the back seat. I smooth it out and carefully save it. Charlie's first gift I think, smiling to myself. Charlie's first gift. I stare without emotion out the window at the novelty. Everything now has a label.

5:35 am I'm still in the dark at the hotel table. I'm choking back sobs now and consider sending a mass text in all caps to everyone I know, "I MISS CHARLIE____" ... I smile at the thought. Is that the virtual way to scream in public? All caps for the scream effect. Lots of exclamation points for the extended scream... Who knows? I smile at the wit of my dysfunctional mind... until I stump myself. How would one textually express quietly sobbing by yourself in a dark, hot hotel room... The light wit is replaced by crushing sourness in my face and throat... I slide my face down into my arms on the table top and cry. My heart is broken. I miss my boy.

10:15am The second day after feels more like three. ... There are moments of clarity and I hate them. I resist the fresh breathes of a Charlie-less life. Our minds stay happily dysfunctional...distracted, confused. We move, we act, we speak only when needed. We don't decide, evaluate, suggest.... Perhaps, we appear to others to be functioning, but the essence of thought is gone. Imagine lacing up sneakers that have no bottom and then taking a walk. Who would know? Today my mind is a soleless shoe.

Day 3 of a Life I Never Wanted

Well that didn't go well. The second day I mean. Who saw that coming? The deep isolation and silence. The resentment I held for anyone close to me who dared not wallow in agony with me. Laughter, conversation, even light observations made my skin burn and my eyes moisten with hurt loyalty. How could anyone breathe, let alone talk in this world without Charlie. We went to Bradley Beach, NJ to meet my uncle at a parade for Memorial Day. I know; ironic. Memorial Day celebrations with parades and music, children and laughter. Buckets of hoopla to help us remember those who have died. Is anyone around me really having trouble remembering? Remembering is not my problem. I remain committed to never forgetting and I don't see any parades or bagpipes marching by to support my needs. Maybe I should start twisting up balloon animals and telling those around me about my boy, Charlie. Yes, maybe I'll paint a sweet butterfly on a small girl's face as I tell her about his laughter or "Mommy" screams of joy whenever he saw me. The wit of a dysfunctional mind continues to satisfy me.

The afternoon and evening went even worse. I'm too tired to even explain or understand. Would it be enough to say I miss my boy and don't understand why my grief isn't universal? Anything other than silence or sobs around me are struck by anger and biting words in my attempt to defend my son's importance. Somehow I think that Charlie would be pleased to see me so angry, so lonely. Am I beginning to change who he was?

I'm attempting to hold myself up to a disciplined, mature grief to prevent further damage to my living loved ones. I am failing. I'm up and running with them, but I lack the understanding, energy, or mind to maintain the position of recovery. It's as if you saw a skyscraper from a long distance or a helicopter's point of view... It seems to be solid, but, on closer inspection, there is no foundation. Yes, I seem to be chasing normalcy with such fervor, but look closer and you'll discover a building without walls.

How did you feel frustration, weakness, or failure in the early days?

Gaela
age 16

Just leaving the gas station connected to an Arby's on our way home from the soccer tournament in New Jersey. It's silent. Right before this gas and food stop my parents had a fight…again. It seems as though the stress of the funeral arrangements for my brother have made my parents on edge. The grief is too much for a parent to bare. There are moments of happiness but they don't last for long. The car ride home is constantly tense and quiet, except for the occasional calls my mom makes for "Charlie's last party" or the replaying of the movie Gnomeo and Juliette which I have probably seen about 10 times on this one trip.

I'm too quiet. My brother, James, always knows the right thing to say to keep a situation from becoming too tense, but he's not here. He stayed home this weekend for his soccer tournament in Virginia Beach.

I constantly miss Charlie. I might not show it, but I cry at least once a day. Ever since the incident I have made my relationship with my siblings stronger. I don't want any more fighting. I can't imagine what life will be like after our final good bye to Charlie in this upcoming funeral. I feel as though my writing is too personal, but I'm not sure what else to write besides what I'm feeling. Hopefully, sleep will being me peace… and more thoughts.

I have yet to dream about Charlie. My dad and Jack have, but Charlie has not come to visit me yet. Hopefully he will soon. I miss him.

My relationship with Jack seems to have strengthened the most. On this New Jersey trip we have sang, laughed, and played games with each other. I had no idea how mature he was "pre-incident". I had always viewed him as just a little kid, but now I view him more as a peer.

He has also become Lola's best friend.

Mom's Journal

Day 4... The Pain Keeps Marching In...

The pain continues. I feel isolated. Charlie is my every thought. Snuggly time, cheerful greetings, his helpful little nature. I feel dead, but worse. I'm the living dead with busy, unnecessary things to do that guarantee I never rest in peace. It seems so unfair and laborious. I seem to crave being busy... small tasks, always walking, never sitting, always absorbed in new ideas and problems. Escapism. If I don't want this new life, I'll do anything to escape it. And it's not really the life I'm looking to leave, it's the reality. I don't want to focus on the thoughts and heartache that are decaying me slowly. When I do slow down even for a minute and sit in a chair or park the car or stare out a window his face is already there and I can only allow a faint repeating moan of despair, "Charlie, Charlie, Charlie....".

While I hurt at the loss of my son, Charlie, I love my other four children completely. They are hurt, damaged, and grieving as I am. They need mothering, comfort, and repair. The horror of watching my son slowly die while Jay and I put the highest and best efforts towards his care frighten me. Today, for now, I fear my children would be safer without my care. Although I love them as I love Charlie, I'm afraid to risk the heartache, loss, and guilt that came with my adoration of him.

Is it truer love for my children to remove myself from their care? Is it more cowardly to avoid the heavy emotional gamble of loving them completely. Yes, I know they need me. Or rather, I'm being told that often enough. I'm not convinced. That a child needs a mother is obvious to even my clouded brain. My children, though, deserve the best of mothers. They are excellent, caring, high quality children. They've became unwilling witnesses and participants in horrific trauma of a devastating personal nature. I can't imagine the shock of seeing your small brother floating face down. It is painful for me to picture my 9 year old son struggling to pull him from the water. My 16 year old daughter must have been frantic as she called 911 and stared in shock through a window at the horror unfold. I can't imagine the disciplined panic that my 15 year old son maintained as he administered CPR to his little brother's lifeless body. My shell of maternity, shaken and fragile, under this tear stained shawl of grief is an unacceptable replacement for the Super Loving-Super Mom who once resided here.

And so I struggle. To be or not to be. Every day the decision seems more critical. I'm breaking apart. My heart feels dead. This scares the children. Do I fight to recover? Is it possible? Is that even the right word? Recovery. This seems to mean getting back to where you were. I find myself today, though, in a life I never had. Recovery can also mean gaining back that which you have lost. That, too, is impossible. My messy mind likes this idea of recovering Charlie.. A_shiny, sweet, baby Charlie sitting on a "recovery shelf of lost items" of the intellectual company's department of mental madness. The madness hurts.

I silence my mind and stare out the window during our long journey home. Hush little mind. For the chatter of noisy grumblings of random thoughts are appearing far too frequently. I've gotten used to being empty, but the mind, however faulty, has begun an impressive rate of thought production. Regardless of the low quality of my current thoughts, they are thoughts and connections nonetheless. Unless I can shut this overzealous mind down quickly, it might stumble back into reality. And then I'll burn with the memories, the despair, the guilt, and the truth. Stay numb. I can do this. Think nothing. Stare in silence. I glance at my husband. "Do you know what's happening?_", I ask him silently in anger. I've leaving the hollow people. My senses are beginning to feel again. Now my time in the hollow is limited and at some surprise, future moment, I'll be joining the Camp of the Angry and Pained.

The Camp of the Angry and Pained...

We left hastily from New Jersey and arrived home to visiting relatives. They will stay with us during this difficult funeral week. We spread out the casseroles and dishes that neighbors had sent. We began to play Irish Ballads of Tommy Makem and the Clancy Brothers. The soft condolences and obligatory hugs were gently given to all… The laughter soon followed. Relatives engaged in the discoveries, changes, and conversations that many months separation from my surviving children quickly prompted. Irish wake week had officially begun. Like a Christmas time family reunion, the energy was lively and the laughter and music sprinkled the room. I spoke through numbed words and carefully phrased thoughts. Something was terribly wrong with this house, but I was not about to tell anyone. I was not able to cause alarm or garner pity. His absence to me was deafening. Wouldn't Charlie have been quick to share high 5s, dance moves, and skip around the table? Yes, it seemed like a family reunion at Christmas time, but a child was missing from the picture, a stocking was missing from the mantle. I was furious and hurt at the levity and story telling… and I sat back in resignation to simply observe. I was furious and hurt and that confirmed my current position. I was now solidly residing in the Camp of the Angry and Pained. This new experience would last longer than I could ever imagine.

What events made you feel angry or pained?   What was happening to heighten your private hurt?

Dad's Journal
Jay

I am so very, very sad. I feel guilty if I have the slightest bit of levity. Therefore I don't talk too much in fear of seeming like I am not thinking of Charlie. It still does not seem real. I feel ashamed for making so many people sad. But most of all I miss Charlie and don't know how I'll live with the knowledge that I wasn't there to save him. I know Elise blames me and I don't know what to say to her because I don't want to make her mad or upset. I try to keep my mind occupied on dumb and mundane things… like how green someone's yard is or whether or not I like Maryland's new license plates and signs, I don't seem to miss one road sign now. If my mind stops processing useless information, then I think of Charlie and I get so sad. Sometimes there is a break in information gathering and I immediately feel like crying, you will hear a long exhale. That means I just pulled back tears. I feel like I push them back inside, (cliché I know, but that's exactly the feeling). I try not to think about what people think about me, I try not to think about how my kids hurt, I try not to think about how Elise hurts, I am sad. I try to act like everything is normal, I know it is not.

Gaela, age 16

Today was the first day of a new life. A life that neither my family nor I planned on living. A life without my brother Charlie. Although it has been officially two weeks since the incident, which means it has been two weeks of this new life, I consider today as day one because yesterday I gave my final good bye to Charlie. It was his funeral. I cried throughout most of it. It felt like a dream...a nightmare. I trailed behind my brother's casket as members of the Knights of Columbus were his pall bearers. To honor Charlie I volunteered to give a reading during the funeral service. Before I read to an audience of hundreds, I was in my pew crying attempting to comfort my mother and myself. When the priest sat down it was my cue to head to the front and read. I wiped my tears and headed to the front. I spoke loud and clear in hopes Charlie might hear me, too.

The Vacation
James, age 15

The day was a short one. I was woken up at 8:30 to pack for a trip that I was second guessing. All I felt like doing was laying in bed all day... but that was not an option, so I loyally did as my Father asked and got ready to leave. I don't even know where my mind was. I was throwing clothes in a bag at random. Once I was done packing my personal things, I began to help with everything else we were bringing to Corrolla. It seems like "we are leaving in 5 minutes" were the only words said... and yet, it seemed to take hours to leave the house.

The car was packed with food from the funeral. I was cramped but it did not matter to me.... Lots of things do not matter to me as much since the day I found out Charlie was not coming home. We took an hour and a half trip to arrive at a home only 30 minutes down from our beach...thanks to the weird highway systems.

The day was an ugly one. Even though we were in a 3 story beach house, the day was still ugly as if the whole world was mourning the loss of my baby brother. With light rain tears coming from the sky's clouds, we decided to check out the beach which also was ugly. The water was cold and the waves were flat. Even the ocean was depressed. After about 30 minutes of pretending to relax at the beach, we returned to our estate to try and soak up some heat in the hot tub.

Lola started off the day sick as though her body knew something was wrong. Her other half was missing. Her mind is oblivious for she still loves to laugh and run. I am jealous that she is not experiencing the same pain as her family. At the same time, I am sad, for I know she will never have a good memory of her other half, Charlie, in her later years. That is why my mom (the situational genius of the family) had decided to record the funeral professionally and have us write these journals. That's so that my baby sister can know how loved her "other half" is, and how big of a chunk he has taken from our souls with his departure.

Mom's Journal

We entered this mini vacation right after the funeral... We've been in a great rush to nowhere and now that we've arrived at a friend's home in Corolla, North Carolina... following great directions right to the driveway, we are lost. What are we doing here? I climb the stairs slowly in silence and stop often to stare at the beautiful photographs of a young baby boy... most likely alive. Yes, I'm certain, actually, that he's alive. I quietly without consideration begin removing them, turning them over, or placing them in drawers. We slide open deck doors and hear the scream of laughter, children, and the rings of an ice cream truck. I hold my forehead involuntarily in response to a constant dull pressure that has taken up residence there. I'm silently grateful to the person who closed out the happy noises and shut the deck.

I retreat to a bedroom and lay sideways. What now? What forever? Did Charlie come, too? I lay in hazy thought staring into space until I realize that the deck door remains open and the joyous sounds continue to parade the airs around us. I discover with idle curiosity that I can suspend the sense of hearing when deep in thought. Nice. But will it bring back Charlie? I am exhausted, but sleep avoids the broken hearted. I am up the entire night. For the first time in my life, I am failing to solve my own problems. I cannot find my way out of this reality. There are no answers I can google or self help books available. Certainly, there's plenty of materials and opinions available for the grieving, but no answer is available for changing the reality...bringing Charlie back.

So, I lie awake all night. Hurt, sad, wondering, panicked, thinking, whispering.... It is maddening and wreaks havoc on the next day. I'm quick to cry and am walking around slightly gape mouthed as if breathing would be easier if air just entered and exited respectfully, as needed, without interrupting the malfunctioning mass known as Grieving Mom.

The days pass like a dream. Engaging, questioning, smiling, complimenting…. But, we all sense honestly, yet silently, that we are interacting on a false, formal, friendly level of family. The nights are worse. I fear the dreams and I suffer from loneliness. I tell Jay about how lonely my grief is… How much I need his help… The discussions don't help a thing. It stretches the gap between mom and dad and parents and children.

The kids seem to be healing beautifully and we spend time daily shoulder to shoulder discussing their progress. As always, Jay and I burst with pride at their maturity, success, and goodness. Jay behaves all day as if he too is healed. He often proudly displays loud laughter, long stories, and the occasional video game focus. For me, I am failing to find a healer, a mother for myself. Jay shuts me out and acts as if everything is normal. He is angry when I ask how he's feeling or whether he misses Charlie. He shakes his head and won't engage. I don't know how to stop the hurt. The kids seem to be releasing their pains and Jay seems to have none. Where does that leave me?

Gaela,
age 16

Yesterday, the second day of this new life, started with donuts. Donuts. Donuts, like my family, have a hole that cannot be filled. Now for us, this hole is caused by the loss of my brother Charlie. We may try to accept this missing piece, but it will never be filled. After our comparative breakfast, we had a beach day. The beach distracted my mind as I played in the waves with Jack. The beach seemed to distract my mom's mind to an extent. Pre-incident, there was no question as to where we were in the water. But, there was a sporadic, "Where's Jack? Have you seen Jack?", coming from my mom. The night later felt calm and relaxed as we hunted for sand crabs in the dark with our flash lights and laid on our backs and looked at stars. One major change my family and I have noticed is Lola's change in personality. She has adopted Charlie's confident, out-going, and loud-spoken personality. We all miss him. Although Lola may remind us of him, she will never be able to fill that hole inside all of us.

James, age 15

The days are getting better. I don't know if I'm the only one that feels this way, But since the day of the funeral everything has very slowly but surely getting brighter. Life was just a foggy, gray evening with relatives saying sorry, but knowing there was nothing they could really do. The day of my last journal entry was a nasty one, rainy, cold, and gray. But today feels different. The sun is shining and the blue sky is wide. There is an occasional white, puffy cloud that I feel Charlie is on, watching the commotion of his family's sadness. I feel like Charlie is almost as upset as we are for HE lost his family, and he cannot share his happiness with us since we are not looking at the bright side of the situation. He is happy and I'm sure he wishes for us to be too.

The air is warm and the ocean is glassy. Even the dolphins are out having fun today. With him on the back of my mind all day, I am going to try to have a good one in his honor.

Jay, Dad's Journal

I am numb... yesterday I started to think about things, I still cannot even write about, and I realized it would make me come to a complete stop. So I turn my thoughts to other empty thoughts. I try to pass time. I wish I could just jump three years into the future because then I can remember and not want to stop. However, I know that my other four children need me to be there. I love them just as much, and they need us more. So I try to be with them and try not to think about Charlie, which makes me want to stop. What a cyclical thing. I will get through this... the kids will get through this... I worry about Elise. I try to keep things light with her. I don't know if not thinking is correct, but it seems to get me through, otherwise I would stop. I worry, I try not to think and I am numb.

Mom's Journal

Desperation. I can do this. I called around for the least expensive wave runner rental company yesterday. I thought, somehow, if the kids had over the top adrenaline fueled opportunities this week that it would lessen the pain. It would lighten the damage. Sad. These are teenagers and a nine year old and normally, I can't see the end to their intelligence and maturity. Yet, in a week of loss, hurt, feuding, and change, I equated them to trained animals. Hey, if we give them extra peanut butter, maybe they won't notice we've moved them to a new cage. Best of intentions meet confused mind. With a wave of my wand the former over achiever becomes the over believer.

Well, regardless, of the mess in our minds, my 3 older children and I gingerly step out of the muck and find ourselves driving to the Soundside Rental company to spend thirty minutes on wave runners. These are loud, noisy, machines that make it difficult to think and impossible to communicate. I could have saved the money and invited the kids to spend some time in my head. But, we're not thinking clearly. We are going through the motions, going places, going on. So we find ourselves racing around a small parcel of the Currituck sound. James and Gaela on one wave runner, Jack and I on the other. We go top speed, we race, we jump, but refuse to get anywhere near each other. I'm sure you appreciate our dedication to avoiding new tragedies before the previous ones have been accurately processed.

We race. One side to the other. One circle after another. Was it fun? I'm not sure we're qualified any longer to recognize fun, but it passed time.... So that's a good thing, right?

We return the wave runners and walk slowly to the car getting our land legs back.... But then, the long haired owner calls out.

"Ya called yesterday, right?" he confirms…. "Take half your money back for your boy. I hope things get easier…easier for all of ya" he says. His prolonged grasp of my hand as he gives me the cash, the catch of his throat as he mentions my boy, and his teary eyes told me what was happening.

My children watched with pale faces and questioning looks until I explained,

"Charlie's third gift" I shout holding the money over my head. "Charlie's third gift." My adolescent zombies melt into wax as we warmly hug each other and hold on tightly as we huddle and hug to the car. I break away just to thank the owner again and get his name…

"Thank you, Bernie", I say with shaky voice… "Thank you, Soundside Bernie__", I scream to the heavens_ I grab a camera and took a quick shot through the windshield with excitement. Another label. The first time I used a camera post Charlie. (It turned out to be the only time I used one as of this book's printing six months later.)

Gaela, 16

Days feel like dreams as nights feel like nightmares. During the day, we seem to have a cohesive, working, positive family. This is exemplified by our relaxing on the beach, bike rides, and even crabbing by the lighthouse. My parents even get along during the day. Little do the people around us know that when night hits, all hell breaks loose. Our seemingly perfect covers are unbound and how we are really feeling is let out. My dad becomes enraged, as does my mom. Both of their furies create a nightmarish fight. Although we are all in pain, I know my parents are feeling the pain the most. Sometimes I am scared. When these fights happen I stay quiet. I don't want to get involved. I'm scared my involvement will worsen the situation. James mutters comments and these grumbles worsen the situation. Sometimes I feel like running away from it all. I don't because I know that if I do, my parents will grieve more and I will have nowhere to go. I also k now that running away would be selfish because I would be leaving more pain with everyone else. I can't leave my family and the pains we all feel. We need to get through this together. I don't want any more grieving or fights. I want things to go back to normal, but sadly I know things will never be the same.

Mom's Journal

The truth is that things are terrible. The kids aren't doing as "beautifully" as I said. Believing that they were doing fine, seemed to prevent me from adopting more worries, more concerns. But they are struggling. Which means we are failing. And now, I feel like quitting, giving up. It took this long to have such a loving, close family. If we all fall down , would we have the strength to rebuild it all? Would we know how? Our first family was formed from baby stage to the present. Could successful adults be formed from angry, grieving teens... I hate existing in the land without answers. We are citizens of the uncharted. No one prepares you for grief. No gas station sells this road map.

I'm desperate to get this painful poison out of me so that I can return to Jay and my children. I can only catch a glimpse of them or the sounds of their voices from time to time floating over this massive wall of grief that dropped between us. I hear them encouraging me to join them. They hear me calling out for help getting over it. But, despite our attempts to reach out for each other, we are unable to see where the other party stands... the wall is too high... And so we reach out and swing our hands to try to find each other. We begin to jump and swing wildly hoping to even find help and find each other by luck. We are not lucky.

No matter how often I call for help, no matter how often Jay describes what I should do to join them, we are too far from where the other side stands. Jay is tired of trying. I begin to panic. If I can't get over this massive wall of grief built with heavy images of happy times, darker thoughts of Charlie's final times, guilty hearts, and fear for our family.... If I can't get over this wall than I may never reunite with any of them....including myself. I may be lost forever in this dark muck of agony. By losing one child, I may lose them all.

I try one final time to reach Jay. Quiet voice…. Children out of earshot and sight. "Jay, how come you never mention, Charlie?" I ask timidly. He sucks in his breath and sits back in his chair…. *Where is she going with this? What is she expecting?* He thinks through tense jaw. I shyly continue. "I think it would comfort me, if I knew you were with me. If you hurt also. I think that if you are here with me in sadness, somehow, than we could grab hands and find our way out together."

He looks off in anger. "**I've already told you I am. I am sad. I do miss him.**", he continues in steely restrained forced words. I push on, determined to finally find him, "So that's it. You have nothing further to say? You don't feel this grief I feel anymore?" He looks likes he wants to throw a chair.

I take a step back. Go gently…quieter voice. "In the hospital, you were my everything, Jay. You led me in novenas, you talked to the saints, you bathed my little Charlic. You made me laugh. You stood up to every doctor and questioned every policy. We made plans and moved as one. I just kinda think I can get back to you… I can get through anything, if you could get shoulder to shoulder with me like that again."

Deep exhale from Jay and I wait…. He goes on to describe the hurt and misery he's been suffering alone. *He shares his following journals with me.*

Jay 6/9
The red camera.
Camera Rojo.

We have always used disposable cameras…even have one in garage from 3 yrs ago…never developed…don't even know where from…..Elise always saying we need to take photos…see soccer moms with their big lenses. Two xmas's ago bought her top of the line camera...she cried with joy...I had researched for weeks....found waterproof, shockproof. Loved it...lost it one easter Sunday on a trip.. upon return purchased identical camera...then at gaelas fl. Soccer tournament and last vaca in p.rico I nonstop took pics....love that camera

 One of the few items I cherish...However, it sits here on the counter everyday...Everyday I see it on the counter, yet I never touch it...I know why...Do I dare document us on "vacation," without Charlie?...Does anyone ever smile anymore...Do I dare catch on permanent digital that Charlie is not here? I can't ever imagine taking a picture again. I hate what that cam can no longer capture.

I don't bring up Charlie to Elise...why? If she is relaxing or doing something and not crying, why would I...When would I...When I think of him? Then I would never be with the children...only crying and talking to Elise. I am in a catch 22. If I bring him up when she is not crying and seems to be occupying herself, then I put her right back into sadness. Otherwise, she is sad, and what can I do? She seems to want to be there for the kids, but if she is not mourning, then she is not being a caring mother for Charlie's sake...she needs to realize that we all miss him and that she needs to be strong for the others. I am very sad for her....It seems I can never be right.

Jay, Dad's Journal 6/10

Yesterday we woke up early and rode bikes 4 miles to the lighthouse in Corolla...It was long and hot. Elise bought the kids some treats and they were tired...Elise and I decided to ride our bikes back and get the car to come pick them up. Lola was in a child seat behind me...about ¼ mile into the ride home, Elise stated she would ride on ahead...I was silent...It is as if she knew I wanted to be alone...As soon as she was out of site, I began to cry..I cried the whole way home...silently. I figured people were assuming I was wiping sweat from under my glasses, however they were tears...the ones that weren't landing on my thighs, as I pedaled up and down, up and down, up and down. The only thing that broke my tears lola –dying..wake up wake up... I panic as I feel her head roll a bit. She must be sleeping, but how will I know? Wake up, wake up. I continue to yell and ride over bumps and spray water over my shoulder until I pull in to the driveway and lift Lola from the seat. I exhale deeply... lola's awake. Lola's alive. I pass Elise in silence. No word of my pain. No word of my panic. Elise watches us pass as I carry Lola up into the house. I straighten my shoulders ... show strength... confidence... she sighs and sits on the bottom step.

Do you feel alone in your pain? Explain why others are suffering this loss also. What does this loss mean to them?

James, age 15

Everything went well that day. The surf was fun, the dolphins were out again, and even my mom would show a little smile every once in a while. The hot day was finally cooling off, and as my family gathered around the living room, munching on some delicious fresh pizza, we decided to go for a walk down the street to a little pond where we were hoping to observe some nature. On our way to the pond we met a little boy who was so innocent and joyful it made me envious. He told us about all of the turtles in the pond that you can feed by hand. We were hoping to see some but they were nonexistent. So we were determined to return the next day to see them. My mom thought it would be a good idea to go out and eat ice cream. So I raced toward the house we were staying in, to try and meet up with my older sister who was already on her way back to the house. I leaped over a grassy bush and as I looked up I saw my baby brother Charlie, holding the hand of my sister and gazing up at her with a big smile. Then I put my head back down and continued running. I didn't think anything of it until I realized that Charlie had been gone for days. So when I looked back up to see my cheerful little buddy, he was gone. I was devastated. I missed him so much, and seeing him made me want to give him a huge hug...but I couldn't. I told my family about what I saw and we all began to feel grief. Tears were in everyone's eyes.

Mom's Journal

Number of days unimportant.

I haven't written in this journal in about a week. Let me explain. First of all, things probably aren't going well on a day that you don't hear from me. Bad days are not necessarily a big prompting for making a written record of the proceedings. I doubt you've ever glanced in the mirror, noticed you were about 20 pounds overweight, in desperate need of a shower, and ran to grab a camera. "Now THIS moment, I wanna remember", you say to yourself with a grin.

Another reason I hesitate or avoid journaling is that this is the true and terrible story of my recent life. It is a true story. It is terrible. It is so painful to believe that I seem to be taking my time in doing so... I almost don't want to write it into existence. My son died. We all know that now. But here's the kicker.... I'm afraid that maybe I did, too. My thoughts, my spirit, my clear and conscious mind have not been in seen in these parts for quite some time.

My successful escapisms are the third reason for the delay in journaling. Busy tasks like driving the car to nowhere or moving objects from one place to another have allowed me to avoid life... and this journal that comes with it.

Today, I cleaned out lots of drawers in the dining room. I got rid of three large bags of trash... from just the dining room. Old slightly broken picture frames....receipts...old tests...school workbooks. Things I couldn't bear to part with before. I'm sure you have many things in your home you can't seem to get rid of either...Take a look around. How many items are never used and/or never seen? Get cleaning_ It's amazing how easy it is to part with a sentimental Christmas stocking when you're being forced to part with a child taken without notice. Maybe it's a way of baby stepping... Ok, good bye stocking...goodbye picture frame. Well, didn't all that just wear us out? Why don't we put off saying good bye to anything (anyone) else until another day, shall we?

Did you notice that I said at the top of this entry that the number of days was unimportant? Well, my little grieving self-help books all seem to predict that the second year of loss is worse than the first. The second year?_ I'm pretty sure we haven't made it through the first three weeks. I'd bet_my life on it. Who counts in years? It seems like an "I Love Lucy" episode where she and Ethyl were working at a chocolate factory. Sure, they seemed to have a hard time dealing with the first few chocolates, but they were getting the hang of it soon enough. But, the chocolates just kept coming.... The chocolates just kept coming...

Just a thought: Should self-help books on grieving even give these little morsels of warning?... "The second year of grieving is worse than the first.." I hate to wave my finger at them because they are just trying to help, but it reminds me of the Karen Carpenter story or any news story on eating disorders. Do you have to tell the audience that she used laxatives or syrup of ipecac? Isn't there a possibility that some sad child might learn something dangerous....

The second year of grieving is worse than the first. Hmmm... I feel that this sad mother just learned something dangerous herself. I had a hard time dealing with the first few days, but I was getting the hang of it soon enough. But, the days just kept coming.... The days just kept coming...

Gotta run... Yes, I avoided sharing why or how the days have been bad... Want some suspense? Here's a hint... When I write again, you'll hear about my new grief version of the college party game "Have You Ever?_" aaannndd… you'll hear about my possible diagnosis of PTSD…and the 3 hour runaway.

The Battle of Grief...one month.

I haven't written in a while and I've felt guilty. Oh, I've had plenty of thoughts and things to say, but it has been impossible to continue writing after the last paragraph I wrote. Doesn't it sound a bit thrilling and upbeat? *"Gotta run..."* Who really says that?_ I have waited a long time to match that mood to continue the story from there. Aren't stories meant to be linear and sensible? Well, *that* mood has never been matched. Nor, could I simply pick up and continue to write and pretend to carry on with those pleasantries and swing to my words. It's as if you were talking to a blind date during a restaurant dinner. He excuses himself for the rest room during an explanation for why he'd like to live in Colorado and a few minutes later a perfect stranger returns and continues the conversation. Not only would you immediately know the difference, but I doubt Date #2 could speak very easily for the first man. I simply could not find a way to continue writing from the last entry of the happy, breathless, "gotta run" grieving woman. She hasn't been seen since.

The survivors of the deaths of dear and intimate loved ones suffer simultaneously from two maladies: flashbacks and aftershocks... When people recover from near death experiences they often recount having their lives flash before their eyes. Now how long would those flashbacks occur? 30 seconds? A minute? Certainly no more than five minutes. For all intents and purposes, can we agree that any near death flashbacks longer than five minutes can be considered mere memories? I'm sorry. There is no cliff so tall or bus so slow that five plus minutes of flashbacks would be appropriate. Certainly after the first three minutes of life flashing before your eyes someone would say, "Get off the train tracks, stupid", and perhaps help you up from where you lay. My point is that the survivors have it worse than the deceased.

One month after his passing, my life with Charlie continues to flash through my mind intermittently, but very often. The obstetrician appointments, the fetal kicks, the sonograms and the staticy whoosh whoosh whoosh of rapid heartbeats.... The first weak cries. The wet, cool, red skin. The long piano playing fingers and perfectly formed finger nails. The little folds of new skin that smell like warm popcorn. The smallest red rear ends. The strange seedy mustard colored diapers... The toddler fingers in my eye. The learning of words. The sighs of baby sleep.

After Charlie passed, I purchased and named a star after him in the constellation that was overhead that night to comfort us each anniversary. Within hours, Jay and I purchased the binary star, the one that circles the first, and named it Lola. Somehow, somewhere, we wanted to be sure they were never again separated. What was the constellation overhead on the night he passed? Gemini.

Now today, I recall for the first time, that Virginia Beach General Hospital plays *Twinkle Twinkle Little Star* throughout it's hallways and offices at the birth of each child. I'll never forget secretly smiling and privately hugging my minutes old twins closely when I realized they were playing the song twice. . Flashbacks of these greatest joys cause the deepest pains.

 The purchase and naming of those Gemini stars was meant to comfort us from the sad separation of the twins. Last night, Lola had fallen asleep downstairs and so for the first time since Charlie's passing, we carried her up to sleep in her crib. Normally, because of the tragedy and the memories in their room, we have brought her sleep with us. At three thirty this morning, we heard her crying in her crib and Jay went to get her. Laying in the dark, I silently realized as I considered the empty crib across from where she lay that we had changed her view forever. While the stars were a touching idea, there will simply no comfort for any of us from that sad separation of little Charlie and Lola.

The aftershocks of death are equally painful. The devastating loss of a child is so destructive and incomprehensible that it is literally impossible to absorb all at once. The impact of that instant realization might kill the poor mother herself. The mind won't allow what the body can't handle. In other words, the death of Charlie is so unbelievable that it's taking me a while to do so. And so I wake…and I stand… and I talk… and consider… and I live. The patterns become easier and occasionally I smile or tell a story or even laugh… and then the aftershock. Just when you are enjoying the day or the moment you turn to hang a towel on a railing and you see his little pants…. And they would still fit him… and then you remember.

I might retreat from the house full of memories and busy myself in the garage and clean… Pick up a dusty bookbag, organize tools, lift a bike. And then there they are… His little blue sunglasses… Worn his very last day… proudly… upside down and lopsided… and you gasp. And then you realize… He's gone… These aftershocks remind you that you don't really understand or accept the loss just yet… Your frenzy in attempting to dismiss them and forget them tells me I can't accept it yet. The breathing gets staggered… the chest hurts… and I wonder, "Where *am* I safe from this pain?_" My loss of Charlie is devastating, but my *life* of his memories equals it.

People assure me time heals all wounds. But mothers who have lost children tell me it lasts forever. Time is an interesting unit of measurement. When the twins were first born I spent months in my room with them. It was literally too difficult and unnecessary to bring them up and down the stairs. I recall watching the Casey/Caylee Anthony story on the news as it was just coming to light. The ground search, the nanny and the kidnapping, the crazy, young mom... The twins and I didn't watch out of interest, it just served as great white noise as I nursed, and burped, and kissed each little finger. The snarly, southern cadence of Nancy Grace would soon send the three of us to sleep...Night after night for months... Today, the irony sours my throat that the story outlasted Charlie. While that is indeed an unusually long news story, I've also discovered a sippy cup of milk under his crib he never finished... and one of his labeled unfinished yogurts on the refrigerator door. I absent mindedly sat with his yogurt and slowly ate it this morning at 5 am. It hadn't gone bad and I savored it as realized sadly, he hadn't even outlived his yogurt.

What have you discovered that reminds you how new this loss is?

Month plus one week.

We're a close knit and private family... We've said it before. So, do lots of people... many families are. But, sometimes people say it just because it sounds nice. For example, consider the cute college girl in your group who always said, "I love football, guys__" as she blinked her eyes and you rolled yours.... Or the airhead who declares, "I want to be a veterinarian because I LOOOVE children."

We're a close knit family and therefore have each suffered unique and severe emotional wounds by Charlie's loss by the following indicators... We have celebrated all major holidays over the past ten years as just the mom, dad, and kids unit. Our Texas parents drove up to meet the twins at the First Thanksgiving and to love those sweet, baby turkeys. And our Maryland folks are in and out for games or family celebrations. In general, though, just our little unit would spend Thanksgivings, Christmas Eve and Christmas, Easters, and Halloweens together. Rarely would it be more than just the children, Jay, and I.... And we loved it...

Gaela, in 8th grade, joined me alone in the doctor's appointment where we discovered we were having twins... We were shocked and whispering, giggling to each other in the dark sonogram room... As the nurse left us alone for a minute, Gaela perused my file and was concerned to read the label in large, dark red writing "2PIP case: requires specialized care"... We walked out on_clouds after the nurse explained all multiple births are labeled and separated...2 PIP? I was a case of "two peas in a pod."

James, Jack, and Gaela would take turns going to my appointments if Daddy was at work. We had no outsiders step in at the time of birth. When the babies arrived, Dad would drive Jack each day to see me, but James and Gaela spent each night in my room. They would hand the babies to me and escort their siblings like body guards each time the nurses removed them to evaluate. The kids would stay with them until they could wheel them back to me. Gaela would push Lola and James would take Charlie. My parents came for a few days to hug, hold, change, and coo and then it was back to our crew.

The first year could be described as that part of many movies that's set to music where a lot of action is summarized in fast forward. Take a moment and google "Talking Heads: Stay Up Late" and play it as you read. Now imagine Gaela making bottles, James taking temperatures on his wrist, running into each other, back up, drop bottle, boil again, rock babies, change diapers, turn heads, plug nose, Jack giving slow swings, twist the musical bear, Jay's midnight diaper runs, patting backs, cheering great gas, singing, one more slow rock of swing, and tip toe out..." Yada yada... The five of us, tripping over each other to please the bossiest, little babies.

The kids would carry them from their cribs, feed them, diaper them, carry them to the car, pack diaper bags, take them for walks and babysit them as needed. They took 70 % or more of all of the twin videos and pictures.

How can one person learn to lift a cow? The other day in Church I figured it out. Little Lola wanted to go to the children's liturgy and Jack always feels too big and embaressed to go to the little children's portion of church. Post Charlie, though, he automatically picked her up and carried her with ease down the church aisles. We chuckled at how large she was with him. Her toes were nearly dragging and her head rested against his as he strode proudly. How can one person lift a cow? The Jack Jack way. Lift it every day since the hour it is first born. You will build your strengths as the cow grows.

Jay can work many hours to provide for us... Sometimes, ten or eleven hour days... But if the kids have a sporting event after school, he is at every one. Outside of weekends, there have been approximately 30 games played every school year for the last 5 years. He hasn't missed one. Have you seen him? He sits in SIBERIA! All by himself or with me...10 yards from anyone else. These games are his children's performances as much as ballet would be, he explains. He doesn't want to miss a thing and wants to prepare for any questions or game complaints they might have afterwards...

On the day of the tragedy, they continued to serve and care for Charlie as they always had... Jack tried pulling him from the pool... Picture his strength in carrying Lola. James assisted dad and then took over CPR as dad spoke to 911. He walked out next to the EMS and Charlie on the stretcher...his final minutes at home. Charlie's departure from us..... and so I recall him escorting newborn Charlie with fraternal protection when he was removed for nursery measurements in the first days of his life. I recall how he asked to be Charlie's pallbearer and arrange that part of the funeral. Today, I realize he gave him his first and final walks in life. Gaela describes watching the tragedy through the window, in shock, unable to move, until Dad puts her on the phone with paramedics. The voice on the phone. It was the real voice she heard on the phone that snapped her into tears and fear.

And then I arrive... Drive down ..... park in street....doors open. The sprint over lawns. Literally, running out of my shoes. The collapse ... and I call for Gaela and she joins me in the police car as we race to the hospital… I recall Gaela and I alone in the ultrasound. 2PIP_ US_ And now… A police car… alone together.. "Gaela," I say through locked teeth, "Call, my mom…"… She leans towards the glass barrier, speaks softly, and secures the officer's phone.. She reaches voice mail. Soon, I enter deeper shock. Fear. One more request. "Gaela", locked teeth, "tell him sirens on, gotta get to him faster.' She again leans forward and succeeds. I enter deep shock and she must now speak for her mother and her brother as we are both admitted. She would shout sweetly and enthusiastically to him over the medical teams' backs. I was being treated for extreme shock and so she would tape my Cheering Charlie words onto her phone and run them back to play for him…. She was gifted with a few staggered breaths by Charlie every time she spoke…. They finally stabilized him with machines and prepared to move him to Norfolk's Children's Hospital. Gaela's service and care for Charlie gift her with special labels, the first to ever hear his heartbeat and the last to hear him breathe…. She joins me quietly on the way to the new hospital. Jay joins the ambulance, so Charlie isn't alone. James must care for his frightened brother Jack….many questions, no answers, no parents.

For the next six days, our children stay with each other, home from school, and care for each other as they pray and wait. Gaela drives them to the hospital for daily Charlie visits and counseling. Gaela and James help each move wires and lift remotes to help each other into Charlie's bed. They take turns, holding his hand, whispering to him, and napping. I recall the bottles, the diapers, the lifting, the feeding, the hair brushing, and the laughter with which they served that little boy. I stare out the window to give their moments some privacy. Jack bravely asks about every wire, every reading, every number on the machines. What do they mean? What is expected? I smile, I'm too afraid to ask those questions. I'm too afraid to know. I smile because he shows the leadership of his father... I stop because I'm *also* too afraid to know what he saw that day. Do I need to know? Shouldn't I? *hmmmm....awful images*

Ahhh... his father.. He lifted him from the pool . He carried him to the stretcher. Sad sigh. I recall him lifting Charlie up and cutting the umbilical cord and handing him to me. A proud kiss through his surgical mask. He lifted him into life. He lifted him out. *< My momentary Personal reflection and head shaking at the power in that>*

Then I think of the elephant candle stick and the Culture Club. Uh oh. Have I been missing a big clue? I have carried my grief around like a big crucifix. I have weeped. I have shared. Jay has been silent and that has angered me... Certainly, this loss must mean more to me... just look at my tears... look at my dreariness... Buuuut....Jay is off to work and jay is talking to a neighbor...or singing to himself in the car... Weeeelllll, didn't his grief leave quickly?_..... But then I remember. Yesterday the children and I cleaned the kitchen. We/I am practicing the permanence of loss in baby steps. Throwing out burned pots, or 43 soy sauce packets, a Chuck E Cheese ticket, 3D movie glasses.... Yep, there they go. Trash cans and then pick up tomorrow. "We'll never see that soy sauce again", I declare.

Yes, very soon, I'm sure we'll all hit that same realization about bigger things and people. Just a little more time, tomorrow, though, we move on to the drawer of batteries and electronic wires. Loss takes time.

Nevetheless, I am proud of our completion of a lengthy job and am startled to hear the clang of the trash cans and bottles outside around dusk....Raccoons? Before I can find my other sneaker, Jay enters with a hideous, chipped elephant candle stick clutched to his chest. Ugggh. I begin to argue with the nonsense of the elephant as he hides it in a cupboard... "It was my grandfathers", he explains. I feel certain it was not... until I see the tape... Culture Club.... 1984? Maybe? "When will you play that?" "Do you even have a tape player?", I continue as he plods silently up the stairs. This is so Jay. Always has been. The kids and I have giggled over the years as he clings to soda bottles that are neat, airline tickets, football figurines.... Now, this morning, as everyone snores for the last hour of dark, I recall how he silently went upstairs yesterday with that Culture Club tape....

Wow. Jay has always had a serious problem with loss and has always been very protective and defensive of his smallest properties... Oh, Jay. How in the world? How in the world are you feeling at this loss of your little pal, Charlie? How many countless times have you searched through garbage, after house cleanings, to save even a broken watch? But, Charlie? Jay you must be broken. You cry at movies. You cry when you hear other kids cheer for your kids. You cry at soccer goals....You cry at every birth. So now... no cries? You must be really broken... I am so sorry for your loss. I don't know if I ever said that. You aren't to blame... You want and fight for every little thing of yours, including that Culture club tape and the awful elephant candle stick.... You certainly fought and must hurt at the loss of your little doppleganger... the boy who looked just like ya. Who would shave each day next to you... Foam up the cheeks... Razor for dad and a popsicle stick for Charlie and you'd shave away together.... You must not trust me or maybe even yourself with how deep your hurt is..... I am so sorry for you. I am so sorry for all of us.

Who else is hurting with you? Why do they need sympathy also? How have you seen their pain?

Month one, week one (for the weak one)

As I try to journal this morning, the light keeps getting blocked out and my mind is distracted as well. A week ago my children started a Facebook page to pay tribute to their brother and to allow them to continue their healing….. Well, little Charlie has well over one thousand friends now. Yes, as I write, over one thousand of the sweetest and most diverse people attempt to peer over my shoulder. And so I clear my virtual throat and begin to read my words aloud to them. I am a teacher and you see no one teaches us about death and the human response. The deep bonds that connect us and the resulting damages from having them severed. They are curious. Some wonder at the experience of death. Some have come to offer support... And well, some of you are hollow just like me, aren't you? I knew it the minute you entered... You lost your son, your little girl, or maybe you just hurt... So you are here, too. But, you're standing on the fringes and curious... hiding a bit, aren't you? You wonder if my loss could really be as bad as yours.. Isn't that a strange thing that satisfies us? The hollow people? How large the badge of pain? But, you're safe here. So stay... but I'm going to ask you to do something with me when I'm finished, ok? Again, will all the siblings, parents, and hurt survivors of those who have passed please stay until the end?

Now, one note for me- something happened, but I don't have thoughts or words for them yet... Note to self: yesterday Lola asked where Charlie was for the first time... A real sincere question... consider that and journal later....

So, dear friends with so much variety and flavor and postage sized faces... I think I know what you want to ask me... I mean you don't know me that well aaaannd you do want to learn... So I think you're wondering…. Do I think there's a God and are you making a difference by being here? Yes and yes. I'll now give proof for both. Some of you don't like God talk... I get it... but, DON"T MOVE. I'll be finished in a minute. Yes, there is a God. Not hope. Not faith... I got it confirmed.... Seriously. It's a long story for another time. The quick version is that some people turn from God when they lose a baby of 2 ½ , 12, 16, or 28 years of age. They are angry. They want nothing to do with Him or anything near Him. I understand... But, for me? Seriously?_If anyone... if ANYONE is going to try and grab my baby while I'm not looking... I'm chasing you. I'm going to hunt you down. I'm going to learn everything about you... So, I did and I found Him and He actually, well, He met me halfway and we talked...a 2 way conversation and I wasn't sleeping. Again, long story, another time... But, I offered you proof, too, didn't i? Here goes...

All organized religions, both Christian and non, have one common thread of thought in all of their histories... That is, "When ordinary men do extraordinary things, God is there." Read that again.... When ordinary men do extraordinary things God is there.

Ready? Charlie Normile. What's that? Charlie. A sweet little two year old who wasn't even potty trained. Sure, some of you knew him and others know why they are here on Team Charlie.... But stop quietly and look around at all of us ordinary people. Look slowly at the faces, places, and people that have quietly slipped in and joined us..... Did you notice how many are here now?_ Over a thousand?_ In a week?_ Look at us connected to each other and to one another and to each other's brother... And we just keep coming... from everywhere___... Extraordinary.... Ordinary people connecting in this extraordinary way. God. Yep, He's here too. Don't religion this up.... Don't wriggle your mind into disagreement like a tight turtleneck on picture day. Just stop for a minute... Your mother's lap growing up... sunshine... juicy oranges...a lopsided snowman made with your brother with a little dirt your mitten must have included......life, your life is beautiful. That's it. Don't be frightened or leave.... But, He loves you. Ssshh... He loves you....

Ok, so if there is a God and Charlie is in a better place, why do I grieve soooo much and hurt and have suicide flash through my mind? (P.S. Totally common and typical, but stupid thought of grieving moms... Remember that, if this happens to you. I'm trying to teach you a bit. And you won't be thinking much or at all when the death and grief first hit you... So make a note if you're worried and leave it in a drawer. It Gets Better. Step off Ledge") . Imagine if you gave birth to the most awesome little boy and he stole your heart and ran to kiss you and laughed daily.... Now, imagine when he's two and a half years old, detectives come to your door to explain there had been a mix up at birth. He was not your child and was being brought to his true parents immediately. There was no baby for you. They assure you his parents are wonderful, sweet, wealthy, millionaires who will give him a life of joy and opportunity. Don't worry, he's in a better place... Would that reaallly make you feel better? Not for a looong, long time.

Now, imagine that they came suddenly and took your child away from the home while you were at the grocery store buying him and his twin mini popsicles made of gelatin so they don't melt as fast in the sun..... and so you couldn't say good bye or that you loved him or kiss his belly or throw him in the air or run away with him or fight these men or lock the door.... So now, weeks later as you recall how much you loved him.... That you literally took steps to spare him the tears and shock of a popsicle melting and disappearing..... It doesn't help yet to hear that he's in a better place....I think that's the best way I can describe it. It doesn't help a bit... Seriously?_ Life was still great for him here... Heaven can't be that much better than a well-loved two year old's life. Think about it.

So, are you helping me by being here? Yes. You see a mother's pain this great does take an army of loving ordinary people to recover. Naturally, Charlie's sudden and searing loss damaged us all. Even our marriage…Shocked? Oh yes, learn well… Death damages all of us; our relationships, our fears, our hearts… our breathing… It's obvious that mom and dad get hurt also… Well, we're quiet or we argue or we hurt or we are together, but lonely…. But, lately, sometimes, as I glance over my children's shoulders as they read Team Charlie, I'll scroll through your words and your pics and your textual encouragements … Sometimes Lola will laugh at the little children pics on your id photos…. And I feel and act a little breezier, a little lighter… But, here is the promised proof. Last night I was running errands and taking my time. Silent, plodding, not thinking and then… without warning… A text from Jay…. 7:35pm: I miss u. *<blush>* No discussion of the text between us later… Yep, hold off on the marching band just yet… but yes you are beginning to move us…. My eyes are steamy with happy gratitude to all of you so far….

Now, those siblings and parents and deeply hurt survivors of loved ones, it's your turn…. You're here with us… but no one but your friends and I know… In honor of your loved one, shout their name, age, and a message to them…They deserve to hear from you and they deserve to be in the present tense, with us one more time. This extraordinary group of ordinary people.

BTW-- All caps and lots of exclamation points are how we textually scream in public… all day.. keep posting those names… caveman had wall drawings, we have the internet….a virtual legacy…. Scrawl their names across the screen… Ready, follow me…

CHARLIE NORMILE_____ 2 YEARS OLD_____...
CHAR-BABY, IT"S MOOOOMMMEEEEE____ I LOVE YOU AND
I'LL TAKE CARE OF STRAWBABY AS BEST I CAN_____ I
LOVE THE DRAGONFLIES YOU SEND_____

Who do you miss? What do you want them to hear?
Scrawl a message. Draw a picture.

July 5… The Summer of Grief Trudging

Sometimes, I wonder… would people suspect that I hold on to this pain longer because I've gotten used to it? Because it feels comfortable? It gives a sense of security? Like a child's security blanket; has grief become mine?

Maybe, some people hold this suspicion. I wonder if I would suspect it of *them* were roles reversed. I've never been one to think things are too difficult. I've often forged ahead through tough times with a "can do" attitude and a supreme satisfaction at how much I've accomplished. The past twelve months could have been the year of numbers… Two full time working parents, three different school schedules for tests and assignments, five children, sixteen athletic practices per week in the Fall, thirteen per week in the spring…one learning how to drive, two potty training….

Yes, I do suspect I would believe I could also master grief and tragedy. Do my friends think the same? Like the old quiz show, *Name that Tune*, would we face off , biting lips in anticipation, and then….

" *I could overcome tragedy in three months, Gene_* "

"Oooohhh… wow. Ok…hmmm… Yep, I could beat that, Gene. I could get past grief in two months_"

"*Oh, wow. Hmmmm. Nope. I can't do it_ That's too fast. Ok, Elise, you win… go ahead and… BEAT THAT GRIEF_* "

Well, shame on that virtual me.

To be honest the last few days have been just fine. I've thought of Charlie often. I've written about him. I've talked to friends and neighbors about him... but, no grief. No silent sobs. No deep chest pains... This has been the longest period of "just fine", I've experienced. We have had a nearly tearless and sobless three days. That's pretty good,right?_ Look at the date again... the first PC (post Charlie) holiday just passed- the 4th of July_ Having three days of "just fine" at this time are GGGRREEAAATT_ *<So sue me, Tony the Tiger...I said it. GGGREEAATTT_>* Of course, I won't hold onto grief longer than necessary. Nobody would.

Grief is your rudest houseguest...sure he's gone for now. Maybe you haven't seen him for a few days (three). But, you know he'll be back. You're just not going to miss him while he's gone.

Grief is just that... the worst houseguest; or rather heartguest. Grief is not merely sadness of the loss or heartbreak at the memories. If you could briefly experience this state fully and personally for five minutes, you would stagger.

Grief comes with physical pains for all parts of the body. Achy elbows, tight neck, hurt fingers, leg cramps, sore eyes... I pass my children sometimes in the halls and I'm lifting my knee as they are mindlessly swinging their arms. I have discovered Lola two times in the past week, sitting or kneeling quietly in front of the toilet, with her head resting on the seat or on a book. She is waiting to be sick again.

Grief exhausts you. I have had days that by 5 pm, I am desperately hoping that Jay will return so I can simply sleep. Gaela has returned to bed as early as 3pm for a few hours. Jack and Lola won't sleep in their rooms at all.

You attempt to be cheery. To set a tone. To be an example. You attempt to create wonderful opportunities for your children to create new memories, bring new fun.... But you forget grief operates with a faulty mind. So, in grief, *my* attempt at crazy fun times for children, sounds instead like,

"Does anyone want to wash my car?_ No, really, you can make buckets of bubbles and ....and... you know, get each other wet... Think about it... with the hose. Do you want to? I'll do it with you.. It'll ... I don't know...be so much fun."

Long pause.... Stares from children... < *Concern? Pity?* > Don't acknowledge, E, maintain smile, they'll follow your example. Looooook slowly, smiling, face to face... wow, Jack's smiling...ok...good.

Then... the shatter. Jack's smile becomes a hysterical laugh and he's saying,

"Oh. My. Gosh. Mom, that was soooo funny. You have got to do that again. That smile. We could put that on Youtube... You'd get so many views. Like the perfect mom, who's really stiff and crazy. Like 'Does anyone want dinner.... I made beetloaf_' and keep smiling like you just did, mom.... I'll tape it."

Ok, first of all, Jack has always wanted to be a viral video... Last night, I spent thirty minutes with him "googling" catch phrases he could use... seriously. Like "Whatcha talkin' bout, Willis?", the Ninja Turtles "Cowabunga", or Homer Simpson's "D'Oh_". He wants to dress like a panda and run between cars and fast food windows and grab the food..... or, again, in panda dress, jump over sunbathers on the beach and kick sand on families as he jumps....all while I catch it on video *<insert your own news headline...i.e. Crazy, Grief stricken Mom and Angry Panda...>.*

So, Jack's opinion of a carwash's fun level is of no concern... contextual understanding: This boy wanted to legally change his name to "Captain Awesome" last year and was seriously, angry for two days at my refusal...Yes_ My refusal to LEGALLY change his name to Captain Awesome. His anger only melted when I bought and left a book of "Ripley's Strangest Feats" on his pillow with the inscription,

"To Captain Awesome-

Boy, do I love you......You're all boy from head to toe...

*and my friend always. Lucky...so lucky you're my son... my boy...oh, boy_*

With love, Momma"

Yes, the book melted the anger. But, not due to my thoughtfulness, or dear inscription.... I remember Jack running to me and hugging me so tightly.... Thank you, Mom. Thank you so much for this book. You really think WE can do something sooooo strange we can get in here?_ Wow. I love you...." *maternal sigh of acceptance...*

The car wash idea officially became a dud when Gaela said, "Jack, leave her alone." *(Yikes, pity?_ Sidenote to wonder/journal later: Why do pity and kindness make mourners cry more?)* and James quietly got me a glass of water and two aspirin. "What's the matter with the car, Mom? Want us to wash it? We'll wash it. You just have to say that."

Grief robs your memory. Words fail you. Simple words. Asking the older children if they would like a bonfire party with friends becomes a wordy mess as well, and they pass. Last week, I saw some of their friends on the beach as we watched James and Jack surfing… They stopped to talk to us. No, seriously, teens everywhere might be a bit shy with adults, but out of respect for our pain, the children and teammates always stop to visit or hug or help. They also were observing 'the beach rule for locals'. Stop and acknowledge all that you know. A universal attempt by residents I suppose to break the summer crowds into smaller neighborhood faces again.

As the friends approach, I jump forward in my seat and offer an overzealous hello…then lower my voice volume a bit and jump right in….

"Great to see you guys. You should stop by and visit with the kids… What do you think about having a smorgasbord? … I mean, you know, a fire thing. You know, a pit that people sit at for talking?_" *<voice volume increases- game show flashback- I'm on Secret Password and why won't this moron shout out "bonfire" so my mind can rest?>*

No dice… They look at me… is that understanding? Warmth? Fear in their eyes?

Silly, friendly, maternal laugh, "Sorry, guys_ I meant do you all want to come over and…." *Go slowly, E, you can do this…* "you know we could… well, our kids could have a small group of friends over, to make snacks to put over a fire that we make and you can talk and …"

"Oh, sure." One darling child saves me. *"But, I have to work."*

"No, no, of course." *I stumble all over now like Bambi hitting the ice.* "No. Work. Of course. I didn't mean now. I was thinking of another day. You know if a group of kids wanted…"

"Sure, maybe we'll have a bonfire this weekend", another child says airily walking away and waving… Bonfire. Of course. Bonfire. Smart child- I'd make *her* my "phone a friend" option…. What was that all about? I quietly write the word bonfire on a corner page of my grief journal and close it up sadly thinking.. Gotta be ready this weekend with that word- in case they really come.

I sit back exhausted at the energy and thought my conversation had required. I look up at Jay with a sly smile in case he didn't notice my verbal disarray. Perhaps, some relief can come from his consideration of me as a cool mom… one who talks to the teens… the tamer of the sour tempered… He looks idly past me at the boys on the boards…

"What was that all about? ", he says with a yawn… "Did you forget my sister's family and my Dad are coming in town this weekend for the 4ᵗʰ of July." *uugggh*

I silently place the beach towel over my entire head and face. Too tired to answer. Too tired to try anymore. Hoped to help the kids a little. Best of intentions. Mess of reactions. Gotta just float for a while… clear my mind. I race to think of a safe topic to focus on and find myself drifting off to sleep in the evening heat, trying to compose a recipe for beetloaf…

Sidenote: journal on this later… today's entry says I thought, talked, wrote, remembered Charlie a lot over the last few days… not true. .. I meant his loss. Our lives, our dealing with it, our current states…yada yada. BUT-STILL Can't think too much about the boy he was in an active, lovely, enthusiastic present tense just yet.... Loss of him officially accepted perhaps? Life without him still unfathomable? Hmmm... tripped into possible pathway out of this maze of recovery... possible roadmap to the "new normal"? .... consider and journal on it later.

And how was the actual 4th of July? By 6 pm, for the first time I can EVER remember, it rained and poured and thundered until well after eleven pm. I kept whispering my thanks to God... I drove through flooded streets last evening muttering, "Thank you, God, for remembering and sharing in my grief on this difficult first holiday without Charlie. Just as the nights as he lay dying, You thundered and rained down in anger and grief. Thank you. Big help. I noticed. Thank you, God. Please just keep this up for one year. One year on every holiday, grieve his absence with me, dear God....and then, yes, just one more thing, actually, God... Tell my boy, his mother loves him and sends him buckets of kisses."

What signs do you take as comfort? What are loving reminders of or messages from your loved one?

July 7th.... To the Hollow Girl

My grief journal has always been like a mature golden retriever. Quiet, loyal, and needing very little to sustain… a calming presence. Today, though, my journal has been a like a yippy, young terrier pulling at my shoelaces… especially this paragraph. I write and it pulls and I delete and try again and it's yanking and wrong…. You see I didn't want to write today. I haven't slept much and I am hurting. My heart aches dully.

I suppose when I began this journal it was to share this time of our lives with Lola who is the only family member who is not aware of what's going on around us…Like a language transcriber or signing to the deaf, I'm attempting to place heartache, loss, disharmony, and emotion into textual art… so that my words may not only narrate but also create the images of today…. The end of who we were and the discovery of what we become. Naturally, this is a tall order for anyone and I receive great support from so many people for my attempts to do so and matched understanding on days I choose not to write.

Looking back a few entries ago, in my grief journal, I wrote:

I *haven't written in this journal in about a week. Let me explain. First of all, things probably aren't going well on a day that you don't hear from me. Bad days are not necessarily a big prompting for making a written record of the proceedings.*

Nobody has pushed me to write or share on days that are difficult… Until now.

I received the following comment on my blog:

The days that are not going well are the days that might help another person who is doubting how they feel. This blog is to help you navigate through this awful journey that we all want to avoid. I am not a writer so I am unable to explain the grief and sorry of losing a brother and father within three months of each other. But your words are raw, true and have so much feeling and emotion. To read your incredible descriptions of grief, sorrow and pain reassures me that my feelings are, should I say, acceptable? You said you are a teacher, so continue to teach those who have not experienced grief yet, but also teach us that what we are feeling is real and we are not over-exaggerating. Continue to share with us even on those days you don't feel like writing on what has captured your heart that day. For some unknown reason I was directed to your blog and facebook page and easily typed this email to you. The Lord has a purpose and wonderful plans for you as you share your testimony of grief. May you feel the love of those who comfort you with their prayers.

And while I began the journal for Lola, it is other mourners like us that prompted me to share them publicly. As a school teacher, we have monthly fire drills. Imagine the ensuing panic and disorder if a school's first true experience with fire came without warning, understanding, or a plan. Well, we the deeply grieving were not prepared. We heard of death and loss, certainly. But grief's journey and ongoing damages to a life are not something most of us have ever studied… and so I share.

You may recall once when I referred to the grieving as the "hollow people". Well, that is exactly who I heard from….

So, Pamela, first of all I write for you today. Remember? That was your letter, wasn't it? You search for more comfort… You deeply hurt… just like me… and perhaps your mother and sister hurt even more. So what are the marks of the grieving? First of all, you used the power of the hollow people. You asked me, a grieving mother with many needs, to do something for *you*....nicely, of course, but you asked. That's one of our marks, I think, Pamela... Seriously. Five weeks ago I journaled,

For, I am one of them...The Hollow People...right here standing before them. Hollow People hold a badge of power. A permission to do anything...an involuntary suspension of insecurities...other people's opinions of you fail to matter. You'll ask for anything you need.

Now isn't that something? So take comfort, Pamela. You're not alone... we have that in common. You also trip over your words to comfort me and explain my importance in making you heal... You wrote,

"To read your incredible descriptions of grief, sorrow and pain reassures me that my feelings are, should I say, acceptable? You said you are a teacher, so continue to teach those who have not experienced grief yet, but also teach us that what we are feeling is real and we are not over-exaggerating. Continue to share with us even on those days you don't feel like writing on what has captured your heart that day."

You took extra care with your words because you and your family are desperately seeking comfort. . I think you are hopeful I can help, but also afraid that I will shut you out. I know. You've been looking for a long time in many places for some relief. Me too. When I read your request to offer more explanations and the timid, kind way that you asked, I compare it to an excerpt from my journal a week after the funeral...

I take a step back. Go gently...quieter voice. "In the hospital, you were my everything, Jay. You led me in novenas, you talked to the saints, you bathed my little Charlie. You made me laugh. You stood up to every doctor and questioned every policy. We made

plans and moved as one. I just kinda think I can get back to you...
I can get through anything, if you could get shoulder to shoulder
with me like that again."

Deep exhale from Jay and I wait.... He goes on to describe the
hurt and misery he's been suffering alone.

We share that second mark... we are so hopeful for comfort, and so afraid we won't receive any... we literally walk on eggshells asking for someone to help or save us.

Most importantly, you are like me and others in mourning because you are willing to help yourself. You seek out answers and ask for help. You're instinct is to survive. That's remarkable and also touching, Pamela.

Now, I'm only pointing out our similarities. This might provide comfort in itself... but, I don't hold any cures. I suppose it's like if you got a tremendously tight, dry perm the night before prom. Having me show up with the same "poodle do" on my wretched head might ease your discomfort, but it certainly didn't remove the perm. So listen as I walk if you'd like... but remain shoulder to shoulder with me as we go... The "face to face" answers lie with God, not me or anyone here with us. He is the ultimate and only source of true and lasting comfort.

The fact is that what makes us human and the delight of God's heart is our ability to love. God is love, and we are made in His image. So, therefore, we are made to love. It is our capacity for such deep bonds with others that makes us human. When we lose a loved one, we look to God. We loved them, we lost them, God is love, so we seek out our loved ones with God. It's logical.

To move through grief with more ease, we must accept and understand the following.

They are gone. It is.

It is unchangeable.

They don't mourn us.

Our time in joining them will be so fast, it'll be unnoticeable... Life will go very fast.

It may not seem like that because time is relative.

What if you had to hold your hand in a fire for a minute? A minute is long.

What if you were going to Hawaii in one minute? A minute is short.

The time you have left in life may seem long.

But the time you have spent seems to have flown by.

Pamela, while you lost a father and brother. I lost a son. The losses seem incomprehensible. But, Jack's former teacher wrote to him this week of losing a brother, a mother, and a best friend... And the other stories that have entered my mailbox are also varying in devastation and heartache. You are not alone.

Here's the sad truth... Some days are better than others. But, ultimately we're living lives we never wanted. The life we loved will never return. And yes we love the ones who survived with us, but only death will reunite us with the one we lost.

Today I simply wonder if I will ever a real conversation again where I don't want to discuss this loss and pain...It remains all consuming. And will we ever again have real, fresh happiness or hysterical, unanchored laughter? At least hope survived...

My advice...

Don't think too much.

Float.

Don't picture their faces for a while... use pronouns in conversation, not names.

Do something small that your dad or brother loved to do or planned on doing... Jack painted dragonflies on our fence for Charlie... painting and dragonflies are special to Charlie.

Sleep and eat well... this will repair your nerves.

Get more oxygen... by running up the stairs or walking briskly or yoga maybe.

Don't live for them. Live for yourself.

Don't cling to mourning family members... My daughter and I try to separate often... Drowning people shouldn't cling to weaker swimmers... Everybody separate...consider friends your "higher ground".. Seek them out.

I hope this helps you, Pamela.... I don't know where you even live, but surround yourself with great people.... like Team Charlie... We all wish you great strength, a sunny morning, unexpected cash in a pants pocket, and an urge to put on bright lipstick and see the day.

What steps have you taken to get yourself help or healing from others?

July 10th… Breaking through and moving ahead

So, we began this journey as an extremely private and close family. We relished in it. It was our trademark. Frankly, though, the size of our loss and the range of our fires to put out required outside assistance. We recognized that within days of entering the hospital. We broke our silence and let our friends know that the children were home and needed their love. Without a knock or a phone call, baskets of bubbles, chalk, letters, notes, dinners, snacks, drinks, began to appear...casseroles, pizza gift certificates, kites... Jay loved one friend's comment, _Hey, Zach, would love to skip school and eat junk food and play video games if James is up for it..._ He was indeed and his friend entered the quiet house and brought air and energy from the outside. All of our decisions and energy was based on the children's best interests...

I remember Jay would limit our hospital texts to relatives and friends. He didn't want to stop holding Charlie's hand. Didn't call because he didn't want to speak about his condition in front of him.... and frankly every moment was a prayer. (A great daily evening tradition we held onto.) Jay was an inspiring and desired companion. We would laugh with exhausted giddiness while our son remained in a coma between us. We would keep each other hydrated and hold off on all meals until we could no longer stay awake. We didn't want phone conversations to deplete our energy or food to make us sleepy... We knew we did everything we could and that was satisfying.

The newspaper article reads from our first few days of journals... while our grief was raw and new. We've come to understand that Charlie's passing has occurred from his fearless, adventurous risk taking. It is because he had such a loving, protected life that he had no fear. Naturally, if we were constantly falling asleep at the wheel while driving or encouraging them to cliff dive; Charlie may fearfully have sat back in life and picked a flower. We held him in a life without risks and danger and therefore, no one is to blame for his curious drive to see more. We loved him. It's better to have loved and lost than never to have loved at all...

But, now we focus on repairing relationships, assisting each other with the process, allowing progression to take place... We are in recovery...We have things we can do and that feels good. Jay has taken the lead on this in a solid, old school way. We are going ahead...as he walks we quietly follow... And somehow we find ourselves last night shoving smelly fish into crab pots and dropping them off our little skiff as the water sprayed and Jack drove, mom snapped guts and shoved fish, Gaela and Lola hugged and laughed on the bow in the water spray, and Jay dropped pots and buoys.....It was physical... It was exhilarating... We were soaked... It was pitch black and we headed home with Jack's flashlight searching for buoys to avoid and the girls and I silent due to the engine... But as we docked, I stepped over to Jay tenderly and he shouted in fear as the boat tilted... _Get the Hell out there! and I leapt to the shore. Sure, he's a quiet guy...but he's got a great point, right? I love him for so many reasons, but this is the cool new one... I no longer wonder how to go forward.... Like a crazy Deadliest Catch captain, Jay was right...Just, get the hell out there....

I'm sure the grief will come back, but we love today and the excitement tomorrow brings...This is in large part to the Team Charlie members who are reaching out to the other children.

Carole Baran,(with help from dad and mom) sent a surprise text greeting to Gaela from TEAM CHARLIE COLORADO, as she landed in Denver with her national league soccer team. Gaela had lovingly packed a favorite and named blanket of Charlie's and a framed photo of she and Charlie for her hotel room. I know the Team Charlie Colorado message was a warm gift. She and her mother in law, who's name is also Gaela (sp?), will also stop by the sidelines of one of her games.... Don't worry, we know Carol's cousin, Beth Hunt; a dear counselor at Saint John the Apostle. Beth is devoted to the protection of all children in her daily job and sent the biggest hearted mom she knew....We are grateful and trust her assistance.

Well, this is not a story of simply grief and loss, but of redemption and recovery. God is love and love is prevailing... Thank you to all of our Team Charlie members who post the nicest things... We read them daily and often... Gaela will be reading from Colorado. Lola asks who's that? And that? And that? Thank you to our local friends....Lynn and Ainsley thanks for always checking in on Lola... Tommy on Jay. Sarah and Jen on me.

It is a journey... How many of you said it would get softer? Well, it is... At times it will get stronger in the pain or return with a vengeance... but we are miles from the first few days of grief shared in the newspaper... We hope you stay with us throughout this first year of first time holidays without him and then we hope to... nope NOT retreat and hide... but to walk with the family that needs us... needs all of us, the most then. Perhaps, you'll follow.

The children were moved to tears to read the following letter they received in yesterday's mail.....

Dear Gaela, James, Jack and Lola

My son Jack was in your Mom's class at SJA.

She had this project called _Letters of Love_ .The children would write letters to a grandparent or loved one every month throughout the year. I thought it was a fantastic idea and I'm sure those letters were treasures amongst bills and advertisements in many mailboxes. Your mom wanted the class to know it's important to let people know you love and appreciate them. It's not a second grade _benchmark_ but a lesson that will improve their lives tremendously.

Your Mom and Dad are remarkable people that aren't afraid to feel things deeply. To go on an adventure, to take a risk, to listen, laugh and try new things. Your Mom loves children- she REALLY REALLY loves her children. She loves you with a passion beyond measure.

At the beginning of the school year when your Mom was in chronic debilitating back pain, she said, _I'll take this over losing a child._ Now I sit in sadness thinking she has to endure an emotional pain worse than any physical pain imaginable. While I worry about her and Jay, they worry about you, their beloved children.

They talked about you guys all the time. Elise talked about getting Gaela's formal dress and about how amazing it is to see the beautiful and competent young woman she is becoming. They cherish you Gaela. James, she talks about how Jay would note how quiet, protective and thoughtful you are. They are so proud to be your parents. Jack-Jack they adore you and your fun boyishness.

When Charlie was failing Jay sent me a text crying, _We can't save him for them._ They wanted to protect you from this terrible pain, but they can't, and it's heartbreaking.

When things are hard remember you are loved. Deeply, profoundly loved. They're proud of you guys, really truly proud to be your parents. There is a down side to feeling and loving so deeply and that is what's happening now. Your Mom talks about being hollow and I suspect they had to turn off a bitof themselves because the pain is too great. I also suspect the hollowness will begin to fade one day because ,love always wins, and your Mom and Dad love you so very very much.

So I write this "Letter of Love" to let you know that when a lot of parents are complaining about their children, or micro-managing them, your parents are cheering you guys on. Their beautiful competent children.

With love,

Heidi Rizzo

Look through your letters of condolence. Tuck a few of your most meaningful ones in this page. Who were you touched to hear from? Who disappointed you? Why?

The broadcaster's "walk and talk"... We've all seen it but, did you know it had a name? The broadcaster's "walk and talk" is when a broadcaster is walking slowing towards the camera as he introduces a story....BUT– he must stop both his walking and his talking at the SAME TIME....usually there is a mark on the floor. They must hit the mark– Get your whole passage out, but not before you get to the mark and not after you've arrived... Nope- walking and talking stop together...

Well, this reminds me of my grief habits from this week. In talking to Gaela, she has similar experiences she retells. Today, with the house empty we decided to journal this together. For me, I am a fighter. I must be busy. I have not sat through one television show without getting up in ages. My time is spent with the children in hopes of healing or on the internet....researching...learning...

No matter how tired I am, I can only allow myself to sleep when I've arrived at an approach that seems best for us. Hope, and hope alone, bring sleep... But, the pacing, texting, research can only end at the same time that sleep begins. There can be no gap between my searching and snoozing...the grievers _sleep and snooze_ if you will. Sunday evening came to a close at 4am, Wednesday night closed at 12:30. The time doesn't matter. It's the speed of hope's arrival. I must feel that I have a plan before I will allow myself to sleep. Prayer may bring it. Or a fellow griever that I've texted.... A website of online activities for 9 year olds. Blogs for teens who've lost siblings. A help chart for Lola's symptoms, behaviors, and solutions. Grief relief spas. Wellness weekends... I will not accept that children who are showing signs of damage will be fine down the road without the proper care, therapy, and follow up.

We are a family of athletes. We have had friends who have relied on an entire army of sports medicine people to address just a knee cap. We get it. Injury takes time and healing to recover. Each injury on the field is unique. Over the years our children or teammates have needed ice, casts, physical therapy, stitches, braces, splints, surgery. Some injuries have permanently removed players from the field due to the intensity or tear. We understand why people visit a wide range of medical experts to identify conditions, propose solutions, and create a strategy to heal. We feel we must do the same as we look at our team of hurting faces. We'll scramble to find them the best care, once we've received the appropriate diagnosis of needs, and we'll attempt to do the same for ourselves. Well. Gaela, is taking over now, but at night if you're wondering where I am... there's a good chance I'm resisting a rest. Get it? Resisting Arresting? Dumb. I know. elise

I agreed to share my thoughts on my mom's blog because I noticed how similar we are feeling and reacting throughout this on-going tragedy. Most people don't know how I'm truly feeling... Most that know me see me as all smiles and _ happy_, but truly I am sad. Lately, I have been looking for escapes in attempt to forget about what has happened and to move on with a much more exciting life than before... these attempts all end in failure. Whenever I'm not busy, I want to get off work because I'm thinking of Charlie...sometimes I'll see little boys looking at the quarter candy machines or I see a peek of a head walk by and I'll have to follow....to see if its him. That's why I understand my mom's need to be searching for relief constantly until she sleeps. Hope of relief is enough for now. I can never stop thinking about him. Even my dreams are beginning to have Charlie in them or I even mention his death in my dreams... and most dreams are actually nightmares and I seem to cry during every one of them.

In my new motivation in searching for a new and better life, I seem to have lost my motivation to do anything else. In my summer assignments and even in field hockey, motivation is lost. I hope that this new and better life I am searching for may become an outlet where the memories of my brother are no longer the only things I think, and even dream, about. Gaela

Have you found yourself staying busy to avoid your grief? Have you difficulty sleeping? What patterns of sleep or activity are new to you?

It all began with three words. "Elise, it's Charlie." The end began with ten missed phone calls and then... those three words. "Elise, it's Charlie." The leaden words dropped from my ear to my chest like heavy sandbags...pausing only to drop my bottom jaw open on the way down. Breeching the protocol of inquiring further...("WHAT is Charlie?" or "What do you mean?").... I leapt straight to hysteria. I thought, "Let's end the nonsense fast." I'll get apologies for the scare. I'll accept. But, my hysteria only elicited further leaden sand bags lobbed from Jay's voice, dead and regretful, knowing the imminent pain they would cause me.

"No, it's true, Elise. He somehow got in the pool and by the time we found him...."

Now, it's gone too far. I respond quickly with a far flung hysterical, "NOOOOOO"...

But, they kept coming... The words of pain and horror. "It's true. I'm sorry."

Heavy sandbags...words in the air... They hit my chest and heart with such a blow that I drop the phone.

Ears buzz... heart races...I cease making memories. My mind takes snapshots. The street. The paramedics... The firetrucks... Ears buzz louder. Adrenaline races through me.

Now I know.

The end began with those three words... "Elise, it's Charlie."

Seven weeks pass... we grieve... we talk... we move... This past weekend we made over Lola's room. No more, Charlie. No sign of him. We think that will help her. We have no idea. We are blind and confused. We want to heal. The pain is tremendous and yet, there is little we can do to alleviate it. Imagine sustaining weeks of throbbing. None of us have ever carried this length of illness. There is a part of us that has died and is irreplaceable.

Blindness. Imagine losing your vision. There is no remedy. There is no cure. You must simply learn to adapt to the new life. I am blind with grief but, not only was I struck with this sudden permanent life change, but everyone in my family was at the same time. We are hurting. We are all blind with suffering. So, we must reach out and find each other.

Without any experience in grief, Jay and I must carry our own emotional pains and confusions while locating our children in their grief. What are they feeling? What do they need? What will best meet their needs?

Each of us grieves uniquely. Lola, Charlie's lifemate, who spent the most time with him thinks in concrete terms and permanence is not comprehensible. This morning, she thought she heard him... "Charlie? Charlie. Where are you? Ok, Charlie...I'm coming... Mom_" she called as she raced downstairs to find her 2 year old cousin who had come for a visit. Studies show she may face regressions in behavior and withdrawal symptoms. Jack has the knowledge that Charlie's death is permanent and irreversible, but doesn't have the emotional development to deal with it. He tends_to show off or misbehave. We have only now realized that this is his mourning strategy. Without that recent discovery and now our parental acceptance, studies show that the adult Jack may have recalled his grief with guilt and shame when he thought of how he misbehaved at times. What else might we miss?

James and Gaela are no longer children, yet neither are they adults. Teens. With the exception of infancy, no period is so filled with change as adolescence. Leaving the security of childhood, they have begun the process of emotional separation from us, the parents. Charlie's death is a particularly devastating experience during this already difficult period.

At the same time, because they are teens, they face psychological, physiological and academic pressures. While they have begun to look like "men" or "women", they still need consistent and compassionate support as they do the work of mourning, because physical development does not always equal emotional maturity.

We, the parents, are exhausted. We postpone our own needs for the kids....

God,

This is so very hard that we ask Your goodness is removing this Cross. Please allow this to be a dream. We know Your son's pain when He asked for You to spare Him the cross. We know Your son's pain, when discovering Lazurus dead. He wept. We have experienced and know more about life and humanity now than many. We are good, kind people who love life and have always worked very hard to honor and love your world and people.

Please allow us to wake from this. Let Jay and I receive new pains and spare our children. They are innocent. They are suffering. And so we, their parents stagger as we suffer from the loss of one child and the pain of the survivors.

If this is our life when I wake, show us the way to walk the path with dignity and successful nurturing of our children.

But, please, dear God, I beg You to make this a dream.

Day after day, though, I awake to the same.. No dream... I rush to Mass looking for God and sitting by Charlie's columbarium box of ashes. Now covered with sticky notes of love... Where is God?

The wounds we each have are very deep and the healing will require us to clean out the deepest parts with God's healing salve. We can't close it off without that inner cleansing....only infection, illness, depression, and worse will leak out in the future if we ignore our proper care today. We sit as a family in a complex grief and I wonder where the healing for such severity exists... Our counselors ask us to consider ourselves in ICU... Go slow and allow the healing...

Then I realize, God has chosen our friends and neighbors as his instrument of healing. Yes, this morning, he scanned the horizons and he saw your face watching dishes or yours starting the car or you snapping the car seat in.... God selected the hearts of pure gold that he knew could heal.... He used the hands of people, friends, family from all over the country to be His voice as you write to us. He sounds like a wise older woman in Arizona. He sounds like the captain of the ladder company. He sounds like the grieving mother with words of solace. We lower our heads as we read your words. Clearly, God is speaking.

We see His hands on earth as you carry our dinner to our door or hug us. He lifts Lola up with the use of your arms. He mows our lawn through your care. He hugs us. We cry when you embrace us for clearly God is holding us. God has legs again on Earth when we see one of you on our sidewalk. We run to receive your greeting. The pounding of the feet of so many teams of runners. Running in his name in races on streets he'll never see. Pounding feet for him. Char-lie. Char-lie. Somehow, without knowing us, strangers find themselves timidly approaching to knock on our grief through posted comments....our virtual bedside of the emotional unit of intensive care. And then with confidence explain, "I'm here to help. We are now friends."

You have fed us, watched our children, allowed us to talk about our loss, allowed us to brag about our boy superhero. You have distracted us with photos of your own. ... Our son Charlie's life was defined by prayers and possibilities to impact people in a positive way. We were crushed at his sudden end.... The finality. But, then you said his name from Aurora, as Team Charlie Colorado hugged my daughter. Charlie spoke to us from Annapolis as so many racing faces huddled behind his initials. You have held his name on your hand with so many bracelets. You have insisted that every "gotta getta a donut addict" in Annapolis, stop and consider him. You've snorkeled and scuba'd with him. You've carved his name into wood. But, most importantly, you've allowed us the time... you've been respectfully distant in our pain... allowing us to shout or hurt before you resume your story or tell us of your children or travels.

We insist on a healthy recovery for us all and so we have opened up our greatest pains. We have exposed these inner wounds which are now vulnerable... But you have silently cared for us. Without knowing why. You return to us day after day from different states and resume your care. You and the gold in your heart were why He picked you. God had a family with a large variety of ages and needs suffering from complex grief, sudden death, and exposure to trauma that threatened who they were beginning to become. God asked you to save us. You said yes. And for that, we are grateful and you and your children and their families will be deeply blessed. What an honor it is for us to meet you, the handiwork of God. Please remain by our side.

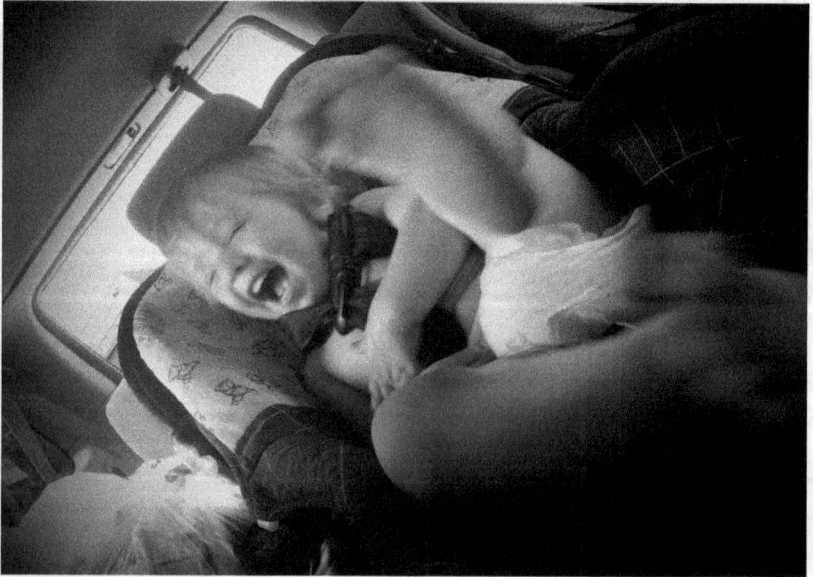

While today is not a day we want to journal, my family has discovered letters from two different people that we share for reasons we'll explain. They certainly allow for a fuller reflection of the process of grief (from minute one in letter one to the present and future in letter two).... Frankly, in grief we discover ourselves victims of emotional "drive bys" . In the midst of casual unimportant activity, we are struck without warning by bullets of remorse. Today's perpetrator was training_wheels. A flash of Charlie's open mouthed happiness the day we would surprise him with a little bike with training wheels...a noisy squeeze horn... streamers from the handle bars. We loved his devotion and proud efforts in becoming a big boy.....

This first letter (just portions of it) is from a neighbor we had not known until this past weekend....

We just felt so bad for your family, and we were in shock too. It was a really odd day that day. The weather was so beautiful, people were outside and riding bikes, gardening, just enjoying the weather. When we realized what was happening, saw the child and began to pray, it was like everything changed. The air was heavy. It felt grey, not beautiful anymore. It felt like time had stopped and everything was happening in slow motion. The child being put in the ambulance,_looking like a perfect child, just sleeping, with beautiful blonde hair. Little bare feet that looked perfect. The child was beautiful, everything else was not. The Mom going in the police car to go_to the hospital, I'll never forget the look on her face. The fear is so intense, I tried to describe it, it's like a fear that I called _white fear_. You feel like everything is fading out and you are so afraid you might just pass out from the fear. We just prayed and felt helpless. My family had the experience of CHKD Hospital two summers ago. We were there for 7 days. Seven **long days. But, we were fortunate to bring our son home***.*

TH... neighbor

My thoughts to her letter are simple… Yep, she captured Charlie pretty well that day. Like an artist, she really got him…his feet, his hair. Ironically, I also feel small jealousy that this neighbor, a stranger at the time, got to see Charlie for his last moments in the fresh air….at his home. .. our home. Sudden death initiates complex grief because it comes without warning, preparation, or final goodbyes.

The second letter is from another new friend PC (post Charlie) who lives close by.

I wanted to take a moment to write you after reading that it's been a rough weekend for you & the family. As you may have picked up from my few posts on Team Charlie's site or from our mutual friends, I lost my son last August. I watch & listen to you share these early weeks of your family's grief and realize I can barely remember those first few months. I thought I would but as the numbness that surrounded our lives those long, dark months, has started to lift, I realize just how protected we were by the fog in that early time. I remember hearing in grief groups at 2 months, I was still in the shock stage & that the fog would not lift for many months yet. They said the 2nd year is often the worse because you are no longer protected by that fog & reality sets in full force. I remember laughing & thinking hysterically…there's no way it can get any worse than it is right now_ They weren't trying to scare me…those meetings are a place for full force honesty…they don't lie or sugarcoat grief there and they tell you ahead of time what to expect in the months & years ahead. They walk with you as that time goes by. As they often tell us _newbies_ it won't get easier but it will get softer. You won't always cry from the depths of your soul daily but you will always have those moments where it comes right out of the blue. We have been through our year of _firsts_ & now approach his _Angelversary_. I barely remember any of those as I tried so hard to paint on my happy face & make all the holidays happy for my other children. I took a lesson from another mom who told me I needed to make memories for my surviving kids, for though the thought would be unbearable, what if this were one of their last years? I would want all those happy memories to treasure. So daily I paint on my happy face & face the day. I watch & see all that you are doing for your children and I know what that happy face hides~I want you to know from one hollow mom to another, though you may not feel it & we may not see the behind closed doors version, you are doing a wonderful job being the best you can. I know...I know how hard that is most days...but you breathe in & you breathe out~one moment, one hour, one day at a time. And you ARE doing it...the best you can......

Our response to this letter is again just automatic and simple... What a shame. What we seem to be facing and what is required of all of us is so tremendous. What an awful shame.

I know I often speak of the importance of the support so many people have provided us. I struggle to express my gratitude for your help on a daily basis and in a variety of ways. To be honest, it is because it is so obviously the truth. To be additionally honest, it is due to the fear that my family will lose the greatest need we have identified through this journey.... Companionship, laughter, stories, thoughts, and tokens of love.... It is impossible to identify how heavily dependent we are on the shoulders of others at this time. We are not ready to discover that either... We are carefully stepping with care to avoid additional losses in our lives- of anything, but especially loved ones... You deserve to know that we marvel as a family how quickly and deeply we have come to love all of you. Allow us your company. Accept our heart's profoundest thanks...

The first goal of Team Charlie was to promote organ donation. We will do that daily. We have raised a great deal of money for Lifenet Health.... Everybody should be in favor of the promotion of organ donation.... Statistically, 100% of people who need an organ, accept one from a donor.... But, organs stay within the geographic region where you live for viability reasons. SO, if you or a family member were in need of an organ, you would hope that you have a region that has a high percentage of donors....

Did you know? Due to the myth that doctors won't take every step to save a life of an organ donor, doctors are not permitted to mention organ donation as an option to families until families ask. This is an altruistic principle the medical field has to build trust in order to save lives... Do you remember the large medical team of TEAM CHARLIE? All of those faces in grief? They would all have to be in collusion together to harvest organs.... Who would bother? Those nurses love the babies... And, again, the doctors are not permitted to ask for organ donations anyways. Once the family mentions it, an outside firm must be contacted to continue the conversation..... We have shared great stories of saved lives from Charlie's organs... We have also heard from the parents of a ten year old boy and the family of a 4 year old girl who passed away on the donor list....The ultimate choice will always remain in your hands.

Well, the children and I knew immediately that a second goal of Team Charlie was to promote water safety... Easy decision. How to do so has been our challenge...

We thought of posting water safety tips... But we already knew them. The kids didn't want people to think we didn't know the most basic things about water. We are in and around it daily.

James also didn't want it linked to the tragedy, because they were NOT responsible and don't want that perception...

Gaela and I thought giving out free water wings in poor communities might make a mad rush of people of all ages... We wanted to make a **significant** difference. So, we thought... Water safety for children... hmmmm.....Safe water for children... and...LIGHTBULB!

YOU TEAM CHARLIE MEMBERS have allowed us to purchase a well in a school yard in Uganda for a small town that only has clean water access several miles away. They often use the local river filled with dysentery and malaria. Illnesses in newborns and babies are frequent. With the well close by, childhood illnesses are greatly reduced because the mothers do not need to rely on the distant water. Most importantly, the school is the focal point of the whole town now, and as a school teacher, I find that exciting!

Perhaps the greatest lesson that we've learned from our journey is the irony of loss.

Grief is both and always universal and personal. Well, isn't that something? We will all endure grief and loss in life. The ways in which we grieve and the progress we make, though, will depend on the will, resources, and needs of each of those in pain. Some of grief's victims will never recover. Some wear it around them with sad satisfaction. An explanation for their dysfunctions, anger, or disrupted life. Some people become severe hoarders or drinkers. Some leave their loved ones, life, jobs, and goals. Life is short. We know that. So how can we deal with unbearable grief in such a productive manner that we continue to protect our life's purpose and beauty?

Everyone of us can succeed and survive grief. Everyone us can return to a life of joy and laughter...but, only if there is outside support and a personal drive and desire to overcome. Success in our defeat of grief, misery, and suffering through loss is dependent on us ridding our minds of regret, remorse, responsibility, depression, or the imaginative, destructive _what ifs?_. We must keep our feet and minds planted solidly on this understanding : _It is._ Your loss is unchangeable. Deal with it. Truly and lovely and daily deal with it. The ways in which you do will be your own devices. Again, grief is personal...

For me, I often look to unusual or coincidental events to comfort me. Last week, I found myself throwing my body down on the beach one evening. The ocean is comforting. There is beauty in art and God has always been my favorite artist. I lay down way back by the dunes.... too tired for the slippy sand shoe walk and too disinterested in the happy family scenes playing out closer to the water. As I lay sideways, I noticed a woman down by the water's edge. She was looking out at the water at children playing. It was clear she was a cancer patient. She wore a loose tank top over a bathing suit bottom and her head was completely shaved. I sat up with attention. I could learn from her strength. No hat, no wig, no scarf... Clearly, able to just own her cross and carry it without shame. I smiled and realized how much more of this I could do in my own life..... Until.... the woman turns to talk to someone in a chair...

What is THIS?!

She has a goatee?   fat belly?_ A cheap beer?

Yes, my life lesson of perseverance was nothing more than an inappropriate guy in a Speedo.... uggh! And no, he wasn't even European! Boy, did I want to yell THAT at him... but I staggered back sandy shouldered to the car laughing privately. Wouldn't Lola be lovely cuddly company right now rather than struggling with the gender identification of beachgoers?_ I mused. Not everything will have a purpose or a reason. Sometimes, things will be deliciously normal... or crudely abnormal, as I recall.

Yesterday, with the SUV loaded with boys and boards, I noticed the back window was still down after they had put their gear in. I saw in the rearview mirror the smallest little dragonflies flitting by the window. I waited until they snuck in before closing it up. I smiled at my anticipation of the boys' surprise discovery. "I let some friends in with you", I said with a twinkle as they looked up at me questioningly. Flash forward 30 seconds... Screaming... shoes waving... grabbing boogie boards... Lola crying in the confusion. Brakes slam 10 yards out of driveway. Doors open. More boys than I remember pile into the street waving the boards and shoes.... And then the two little dragonflies or, in actuality, the longest, fattest hornets flit past Lola and out the door.

"You did that on purpose?", the boys demand. I can only sigh. The explanation would bring their pity... Pity brings tears. So, I simply shrug my shoulders... _Wasn't it you who always loved bees, Jack? Hmmmm.... No? Must have been someone else. That's fine. Back in the car._ Calm voice, well done. Believable. "Mom, what else do you think I like?" Jack asked as the ride resumed.... I smiled at his potential fear of finding a pillow full of slugs with a love note from mom.

Note to self: men in speedos... threatening wasps... eye check: schedule one asap

Well, I guess sometimes we fail to comfort ourselves and it's then that I remember the Hurricanes and Nor'easters that threaten our coastal town. After the most recent one, James and Gaela joined dad in dragging branches and cutting down damaged trees. _How come all of the trees don't fall? Even the same kind of trees had some split and some bend and bounce back._ Gaela observed. _It's the roots_, Jay explained, _trees with a long and solid root system can stand and survive through the worst storms._ There you have it.

For those without grief or loss, remember it is universal. It will come to you, too, one day. Examine your root system. Reach out and get involved in your church, community, synagogues, charities, and neighborhoods. Support and be active in your local schools. Meet the other parents on the sidelines. Do good things for others. Get close to them.

For our Catholic family, a former student's mother from St. Johns emailed me a letter of support and encouraged me to read more of the grief of Mary who also lost a son through no fault of His own. In doing so, I relearned that as He lay dying, He turned the comfort of Mary and her responsibility to one of His closest friends....St John the Apostle. Even in typing that, I am well aware of the pictures, cards, jokes, the funeral, the meals, the silent free lawn mowing, the lift that St. John the Apostle did in fact provide for me in my grief. Now that I take as a true and real comfort and sign.... take that speedo man_

As St John the Apostle school prepares for its tenth anniversary, I recall sitting on bunkbeds in the first principal's beach house selecting textbook series because the building had yet not been completed. The coworkers, the students, the parents, the parish have rooted me solidly and so when the wind blows and, in our case, the bough breaks, I bent low and I feared greatly and I hurt deeply, but my family is the surviving tree's story for the roots we have each built with all of our activities, teams, clients, classes, offices, and ages....

Here is the letter that I recently received....

Hi Elise,

You and your family have been constantly on my mind_ We just got back last night from a family vacation to Italy. It was the most incredible trip to have as a family. Each and every day was better than the one before. History is tucked among progress and beauty, and cathedrals and saints permeate the land. We took with us our Charlie's Angels braclet and throughout our trip prayed over where to put it and to which saint we would ask to look out for Charlie and for your whole family. I really thought St. Peter's Basilica would be the place because the braclet visited many, many churches of high importance throughout Italy and I just never felt that we had reached the place for the braclet. While in one of the museums in St. Peters, I saw a large picture of Pope John Paul II that moved me deeply and brought your family to my mind and my heart. The picture was of the old, broken pope, barely able to move about on his own. The inscription below the photograph said _Strength in Weakness_. I can't tell you exactly how to apply it, but I think it's true. St. Peter touched my heart when we visited his tomb underneath St. Peter's Basilica. Two days later we visted the church called St. Peter in Chains also in Rome. Behind the alter is a glass case containing the actual chains which bound St. Peter. I don't know why, but I felt this was the right place. Maybe because the chains didn't hold Peter, just like the water didn't hold Charlie. I can't be sure why, but I knew this place was right. We prayed to St. Peter and asked him to watch over Charlie, and also to intercede for the strength and determination of your family.

We love you all and think about you often. We are a short boat ride away....come any time you, or any combination of you, need a change of pace...our dock is always open :)

*I hope to see you soon_*

Love, Michelle Clough (and Shelton, Trey and Morgan)

My family and friends I knew would always be there...They are beautiful reflections of what friends and family were intended to mean. Facebook world family you delighted, surprised, and joined me...and I was startled at my need for you. But St. John the Apostle school and parish, you have humbled me to steamy tears... Yes, Caroline Esposito, I just opened the door to Lola's new doll for her to Mommy, the brownies, and pizza gift certificate. You each honor Saint John himself by your devotion to those who grieve. May many blessings be your own rewards. Jesus Himself would approve of your care with loving satisfaction.

I wish each of us luck in continuing to nurture our children and deepen our roots in larger families that we belong. May you understand your personal needs to discover the puzzle for which you fit.

What groups in your community do you belong? Who would you feel most safe or comfortable spending time with in your grief?

Have you ever been to a party and find yourself in a spontaneous conversation with someone that you don't really know. Perhaps you overheard a topic you felt strongly about and joined in. Perhaps, they returned to your group in mid conversation. You talk and wait. If this is a brief exchange, you'll move on... look for your spouse... or a glass of wine... or one of those beefy things the waiter doesn't seem to bring around often enough... Is he paid per hour? He should really be paid by how many beef things we eat_... That would get the boy hustling, right?

Sometimes, though, we connect with a person in a random conversation. Strong agreement. Deep appreciation. Children of like ages. At some point, we decide to extend our hand, introduce ourselves, and invest more time... maybe find a seat. This new friend is better than beefy appetizers.

And so are you. So now today's sun didn't set without you getting at least one kind compliment....You, kind new friend are better than great food. I have felt badly about not writing in the last few days. Your words of support are comforting, honest, and spot on sometimes. You wouldn't mind if I chose not to write. I must. I had intended to simply give my facebook friends a one month update on how our family was. We had received a lot of support and returned minimal communication.... And so we all shared a journal entry to express how we were doing. Somehow, though, in cracking open my front emotional door a bit on that day and posting our journal entries... I spied a friend or two shouting cheers, and holding signs of encouragement. I logged off. Strange. Where did they come from?

No one else in my family bothered to post their future daily journals... but I was curious... and I threw another journal out the door of facebook and hesitated before closing the door. Certainly, there must be at least 30 people responding and shouting... I logged off and stared at the wall.... "You can do it", a_stranger had textually shouted_as I shyly shared my pain. I glanced back at the page later…a crowd was forming… Oh no… "What am I gonna do with all of those people?", I wondered… They would textually throw out kind words, suggestions, locations, personal stories… I shook my head and rejoined them for a bit and they listened more. They assured me I was moving and helping and healing, although I couldn't be sure. Doubts and fears of a new life were outshouted by these textual pals, neighbors, and strangers…. and as I spoke, I drained…. The Little Engine That Could…. can I?

Well, my community of supporters who have mothered my children with praise, and kindness and chatted with each other socially have somehow stood shoulder to shoulder to be the village that this grieving family needs. This lovely group of postage sized faces, hurting hearts, and maternal voices have quietly allowed me to release steam and push forward and release more steam and discover even more and let it out across each sentence. I am not sure of the outcome of any of this, I am sure that my Team Charlie friends brought hope. And that's exactly what I need… Hope makes me tie on my running shoes. Hope makes me excited… and most importantly, hope makes me take the steps and start walking. The steam engine… I think I can, I think I can… Hope might very well help belief to show up. Once belief is here, I can sprint. We all can. I'll gather this family up and start running towards joy and easier times.

God, of course, has always been here. He's literally the only friend since grade school I've kept in touch with (sorry old pals, I'll try better)…. so he knows. He sits and watches. He knows my adoration and shares my humor. We both know I must simply trust Him and then live like I do. We worry though because, it is the human entanglements of trauma, attachment, fear, adrenaline, stress, sleeplessness that will require human answers and friends to get through… So today, my grief counselor says as we close, "Do you have a great group of friends? Have you been able to open up to them?" (50 states and 1,000 plus faces, countries)

Who are your closest friends? Has any individual, family, or group delighted you with support that you weren't as close to before? Have you felt your evaluation of friendships change? Who have you lost? Who have you gained?

Saturday, September 03, 2011

Good morning, Labor Day weekend. When did you get here?

Seasons are always connected in my mind to change. The spring weather brings the first rays of sunshine and little buds to the trees. On one of the first sunshiny spring afternoons, the children and I always take a sun "bath". We've done this for about ten years. We spread out blankets and lay on our stomachs or backs in silence. On our stomachs, we can examine little life in the grass… ants running. New grass blowing. A lady bug taking flight. On our backs, we can stare at the clouds and breezy tree branches. It is our first time in months that we actually stop and spend time outdoors instead of running to the door and stomping the winter off our boots. A chance to stop, think, look.

Memorial Day brings summer. Is any season more closely linked in our minds to children? Can you think of the word summer for very long before you picture little boys and girls delighting in the outdoors? Memorial Day for us this year broke our hearts. Our son and sonshine, Charlie, left our lives suddenly and traumatically. And like a broken bone, our hearts will heal in time and with continued care… We'll always have flair ups or painful experiences, but healing has certainly already begin.

Today, I simply must textually kiss the ground for our family's safe arrival on Autumn's doorstep. I can't believe we made it through this first season. I am so amazed at how far we have come. Thank God we are intact. Thank God we are moving, making plans, looking ahead. At the first realization of Charlie's loss (BTW: a symptom of those who have lost a loved one is to rarely or if ever use the "D" word. It is simply a word your mind and mouth have trouble forming)... But when this all began, our family was a shell. I did not make very many memories of the early days. It affected vision and hearing. I remember our surprise at how often we would trip, hit our heads, kick a table... Literally our vision was slightly impaired. We lost money, keys, forgot dates, information,appointments... Our minds had pulled a fuzzy curtain down and we didn't even know it was there. We were functioning, rising, walking, sleeping but, our minds had started to close off certain corners, certain functions to prevent further pain and damage. Confusion at our confusion was common. Why can't I remember where it is?

The hollow people.

We've learned that the mind won't allow what the body can't handle. I suppose the sudden and immediate loss of our son Charlie was an emotional violence. It's as if gunfire and bombings bore down without warning on our quiet home. Adrenaline raced through our mind's home shutting doors, windows, entry ways. Keep the pain out...Push against the door. Lock. Secure. Feeling a bit stuffy, kids? Deal with it. Look outside... We can't open the windows to that_ And so our minds stayed stuffy and our thoughts were hollow. Nothing could come in. Like being trapped in a warzone, we had very little contact with the outside world. We panicked. Where did this come from? What's happening to our home? How long will this last? What should be do? We stayed in. Spent time with each other. Assessed the damage. Tended our wounds.

Imagine if several dogs were locked in a car together. They would snarl and snap at each other. They would be angry, maybe frightened, and take it out with bites and yelps at on one another. We were the hounds of grief. We were the snarling and snapping canines. We would fight with one another. We would speak angrily. Inevitably, as time marched on the locked dogs would settle into peaceful times. It's calmer and easier for them. They are tired of fighting. Those other dogs didn't put us in here. They are locked in too. And so we also have settled into peaceful times. We are soldiers of the same loss. It will be a lifelong battle. There will be peace but, now we understand there will always be flare ups, pain, and sorrow. We are grateful for each other's company... Charlie's veterans.

We began to receive outside information about our raging battle. Letters from other war veterans who had lost loved ones appeared. 39 years, 22 years, 5 years of battling loss... , 43 blog replies, multiple facebook friends who had loved and lost, and 322 letters of death's survivors came to our mailbox. Soldiers of their own grief. Their experiences and stories broadened our understanding. Their regrets, their traditions, their triumphs helped us create and maintain our battle plan. They were strangers but, priceless help in our time of need...

Jason Feuerhahn   Tuesday, 7/19/11, 5:30 PM

38 years ago my aunt and uncle lost their first child, a 3 year
old boy named Eric, to a drowning. They manage to comfort
each other thru very tough times, move forward, and keep Eric's
memories alive. Their pain slowly eases. They are my heroes.
Jay, Elise, James, Gaela and Jack you have gone to a dark place
that I am extremely terrified of. I know you will have the strength

to come out of this place and to pull each and every one of your family members out with you. Anytime your family falls back a little, keep fighting. Your strength and ability to pull yourself and your family out of such a dark place, makes you my hero. Keep each others heads up, move forward, and forever keep Charlies beautiful memories alive in your hearts, your pain will soften. The blogs you are doing for Lola is what I wish my Aunt and Uncle would have done for me, my sister and cousins. Your blogs will keep Charlie's life real for her. Lola will never be the youngest child and she will always be a twin. I applaud you. Go team Charlie.

Stephanie Duran Saturday, 7/16/11, 6:02 PM

I am so glad that Team Charlie is up and running, I am still working on finding an outlet for my grief. May God continue to bless you Elise. I am sorry I was unable to attend Charlies wake. Grief is so over whelming. XOXO

Lisa Thursday, 7/14/11, 8:15 PM

I lost my mom 18 years ago tomorrow, July 15th. Although my mom never got to hug her nine grandchildren, I know that she is enjoying hugging your Charlie. I think of your family often and say a prayer for each of you.

Ann Stair Wednesday, 7/13/11, 7:46 AM

I lost my mom to cancer 20 yrs ago in Sep. She was only 43. My sister just passed 2 yrs ago of the same cancer, genetic. And now my 4 yr old cousin has had cancer for 2 yrs now. I am very excited though because they are in Cincinnati this week, they are from Massachusetts, and we are going to Cincinnati to see them, a 4 hr drive...not far at all to see family. I have not lost any children, thank the lord, so I can't imagine your pain but I think you are the most strong and inspirational people I know. Thank you for sharing.

Christie Evans Gates NC 7/12/2011
I tried to watch the opening video. I just couldnt. He is a beautiful boy, reminding me so much of my son I also recently lost, and who also is an organ donor...who also drown in my yard, leaving 4 other siblings. I understand and can relate. But, arent we so lucky to have been blessed with angels? Giving so much of themselves even after they're gone? We should be very proud of them. I am reading the book Heaven is for Real and wanted to let you know, it is helping me deal with the lack of closure of saying goodbye and may help you too. We dont live far from each other and I would love, if you ever are able, so sit and share our sons with each other.
It kills me, but I really do love talking about him, he was a hoot.
Be well, and best of luck and thanks for all your efforts in Charlie's name...
I would love to help however I can Much Love and Dragonflies
Christie

Leigh Glover

Elise, Jay, Gaela, James, Jack and Lola, I am so sorry for your loss. I lost my brother when I was 3. I remembered him and my life before and after he was born. He was my best friend and i adored him. I have never met a more perfect loving person and I have come to realize that he was only on loan to our family for his short life. He touched everyone with his smile, his joy. He was so full of mischief to this day i miss him. (i am 54) Sadly because i remembered so much of him i felt his loss like a knife to my chest. Sometimes I couldn't breath and sometimes I wished I had died instead of him. I suffered his loss along with my whole family. I have had a constant fear all my life of losing one of my own children. This is to mom and dad you are so commendable for your courage to face this together as a family. I admire and encourage your honesty. Unlike your family not only did I lose my brother many years ago but I also lost my parents. Their grief was so deep and so hard for them to deal with that i was set aside. I was part of his memory. We never spoke about Ricky's death. It's as if he never existed. Sometimes I would sit and yell at them in my head. Do you remember me? Thank God you have chosen a different path. I know it is not the easier of the two. I guess I should get to the good part. I loved my parents and I had a good life. Yes I struggled with my feelings and went through some hard times but I came to realize they handled it the best way that they could. I envy your closeness and I hope that you all are able to pull together and be as one again because even though I didn't have the easiest life after my brother died I did appreciate that I had one but I think how much easier it would have been if all of us could have embraced each other and our loss together. Good Luck and God Bless You AllSunday, 7/10/11, 12:12 PM

Nicolle Ashby

Elise & family, I feel like I know you all so well already, not just because our families walk the same road, but through the stories of the many friends we have in common, especially within the soccer community. Gaela & James, you are facebook friends with my daughter Caity..while not close friends, you share much in common now and all 3 of you amaze me with your strength & love. It is not easy being the siblings at this time..I know you must sometimes feel like you've lost more than just your brother. Hang in there sweet ones...we parents know & thank you for taking over when we can't.You are our angels here on earth. This road is a bumpy one but you all have managed to find some sunny bypasses...keep looking for those when you've gone through the long dark tunnels. They sometimes seem so hard to find but they are there..right around the corner and oh, the smiles & happy tears they bring__ I think of you all daily..I think of Charlie daily & I picture our two boys on that big soccer field in the sky. Both of them left wonderful gifts behind through their LifeNet donations..they live on in many. What a wonderful job you have all done keeping Charlie's memory alive for all to know him~it's all we want~for our children to be remembered. Elise, our meeting was a brief one, I hope we can meet again one day soon..I would love to talk & share with another that truely understands the path we walk. Many hugs & much love to all of you

Mary Roberts

I don't know about you (Mommy) but I never see my two sons in my dreams. Instead I find pennies from heaven everywhere_ Twice in the past month, I saw a red cardninal fly in front of me. Back in May (Randy's 2nd anniv. in Heaven) I asked Ra...ndy to send me a sign that he was watching over us. I work for Stihl Inc. and a week later at 4am a red cardninal came inside the plant and flew down around my machine. It circled above me twice and flew away. Yesterday, I saw him again while in my truck, waiting to go inside to work. Thanks for asking Charlie to tell Jesus to comfort us. We all need Him. Have a Bessed day and please know that I am praying for Peace and Comfort for you and your family.

My sister, Lisa Vann, and her family, along with the Hendersons, have shared with us, your loss. Even though you do not know my family, you have been in our hearts and thoughts everyday. We just read the beautiful journal entries of your family, and I only wish I had thought to do the same in the minutes, days and months following my dad's passing. We lost him a few years ago, very suddenly and unexpectedly, and I worry each day that my children and nephews will never really understand what a gift they had in Dad everyday. I am not equating your loss to that of my father,in any way, but I found myself relating to a little piece of what everyone said in their journals. I wish for you strength in your journey ahead. I hope to meet you some day just to hug you and to tell you that you are inspiring to me and my family.

Much love to you all,

Shannon Holley Nicoll

We have begun to realize that this sorrow will last as long as our memories. I think we imagined an end. A return to what we were... Despite the pain, despite the loss, despite the value and weight of little Charlie in all of our hearts, I think we had just assumed that at some point we would get back on track. Some date on the calendar would find us talking, laughing, and moving as we always had. What else could there be? That life was all we'd ever known. The people we were was all we'd ever been. We weren't rushing, pushing, or considering this much... But, yes, we all understood and waited for when we would all be back to the place and people we were.

Now, it is beginning to dawn on us. That Charlie's loss changed each of us forever. Our decisions, our values, our fears, our goals.... It will be an ongoing adjustment as we rediscover ourselves and learn more about the changes taking place in each other. Increased confidence. Determination. Today matters. I will speak up. I will speak gently. Heightened sensitivity. Changes in goals,directions. We accept it all. We are too worn out after three months to even grieve the loss of the family we were. We are simply determined to make changes and lives that matter, that support others, that leave footprints...Our new life came because of Charlie and so we dedicate it to him.

In doing so, we want our lives and experiences to show his legacy and loss were accepted as a gift not curse. He died before he sinned. He left before he felt jealousy, embaressment, self consciousness... We journal these words and reflect on ways we can reduce these feelings for ourselves. He never hit anyone, excluded anyone, or hated anything. We vow to have this true about each of us. He was ready to dance, sing, and laugh. His face lit up when he saw his family. He ran to us. We type and post these on a wall. We can do them also. He missed us when we left. He hugged us, sat on our laps, held our hands, pulled us to fun times... Asked us to play, climb, and see saw.

We can be Charlie to one another. We can do those things. He loved learning. He always asked questions. He squatted or pushed his face close to see things close up. We want to feel that again. We want to recapture that age and enthusiasm. We vow to keep learning, to open our mouthes in awe, and to be amazed at huge things.

He happily sang out the family member's name who entered the room as if it had been weeks since he had seen them. He smiled… He gave so many kisses…Done, done, done. He listened to what we said. He asked What? Or Huh? Again and again and again until he understood… before he assumed…before he answered. We must do this for each other. We must be sure we understand and not simply hear or think we do.

We spoke slowly to him. We answered every question. We held his hand. We walked soooo slowly. We smiled back. We ran to him. We held out our arms with our faces lit up. When was the last time we did that to each other?   Does your face light up when you see each child? When you see your spouse? Do you stop everything and run your children as you did when they were toddlers? Hug them? Open your arms? Swing them?

 We did this for Charlie because he was doing it for us. So we want to be excited when we see friends or family. We want our faces to light up. We want to be excited and smile and hug. Perhaps, we will teach others as Charlie taught us, to be excited and show it in these same ways when they see us.

So we've made it to autumn. We are nervous about the battles and heartache we will face ahead.   A birthday for our twinless twin… a missing Christmas stocking. Perhaps a letter from the organ recipients. A mean word or joke about our loss heard in the schoolyard. A Charlie sighting in a crowd. Memory pinches.

Sorrow twinges… But, we are also excited and delighted. We've survived and thrived. We are surrounded on our streets, in our schools, in the stores, on the internet, on teams, and in Church by all of you… our support…our strength… our team… TEAM CHARLIE. God has blessed you often this summer for your comfort of the grieving. You fulfilled his best intention. Stick around and join us as we "Humpty Dumpty"… which means- join us in "having a great fall".

We'll always remember this first painful season as ...

The Summer of Dragonflies!

The dragonfly may remind us of Charlie forever, but your many dragonfly sightings and stories remind us always of your comfort to us all….. We love you… and read your words again and again more than you know… Your pages have been printed and your letters boxed. They are on our chairs in the gazebo- Charlie's castle. You have been read and shared amongst us on many recent nights.

Please stay with us as we continue our goal to spend our first year without Charlie with all of you, Team Charlie…

A special, personal thank you for allowing me to continue to mother my boy, my Charlie, through your company and kindness. You are beautiful people and I am so grateful for your care and protection of my children and family. I pray for your needs nightly. I am humbled. Love, Elise

Grief is Universal, Pain is personal

After writing that title phrase I realized why so many parents who have lost loved ones have reached out to us...even if we were strangers. While we may respond or experience the pain in different ways or through different symptoms, the grief itself is identical. We are experiencing an emotional amputation so great that it mimics and nears the pain of a physical amputation. For mothers, the child was literally born of us, breathed and ate through us, and was the maternally dependant hand holder and lap sitter for the child's opening life chapters. The loss of an offspring is something nature doesn't intend and so for which the heart fails to prepare.

A physical amputation may not be as painful as feared because intense adrenaline and shock course through the body throbbing around the heart to prevent further pain or damage. It is in the recovery and healing of an amputation that acute and severe pains occur. In recent weeks, since the loss of Charlie, we are beginning to have the shock peel away from our heart's defense and acceptance is taking up residence. The throb of heartache and loss is acute and many steps we take internally resound his name, "Charlie. Charlie." But the risk of shock is gone. Panic and despair never even stopped by. Our Charlie thoughts are healthy thoughts as we consider ideas for a tributary birthday or recall special memories. Tears still flow at times but, tears are like an emotional spa. They slow us down. They tire us. We feel gentle after the sourness has left our throats. Tears move us to mother ourselves... to journal, to make a special dessert, to be lazy, to lie down. While they come less often, our tears are like snow days for school teachers. We may not have expected them or even hoped for them, but we are going to take advantage of them and stay cozy and slow down since they came to us all the same.

We had created an external memorial in our gazebo for Charlie... A visiting room if you will. A play room for Lola. While we expect the cozy retreat will bring us great comfort in days to come; especially holidays or grieving days, we've spent very little time in there just yet. You see Charlie is all around us inside our home. His training potty, pairs of shoes, wall scribbles, photographs... I even had a shirt or two show up in the laundry yesterday... three months later. I privately and proudly snuck some favorite shorts of Charlie's into my drawer as comfort a long time ago. But, as I deliver clothes or pack up summer items, I realize my idea was a common one. Every one of us... EVERY one of us has Charlie packed into little corners of drawers or on shelves. I discover pajamas, mini trucks, sweat shirts, tiny socks hidden in each person's room. I'm delighted at their ability to mother and comfort themselves in this small way. This morning I organized and packed a little soccer bag for Jack Jack with his uniform, shin guards, and cleats. Sometimes he carpools with a friend to practice and gets changed at their home. I smile at the last minute discovery of finding it was Charlie sized soccer shorts in Jack's drawer I was packing and not his own... I laugh at the imaginary, disapproving glances of the team soccer moms thrown Jack's way had he run across the field in the tightest, mini shorts his bottom would accommodate. Adidas granny panties.

I tuck each person's Charlie treasure back into the drawers. There will be no discussion about them. I, too, have my Charlie tokens. Memory sparkers, if you will. My first instinct is to pity my family. To pity myself for hanging onto these barely tangible pieces of Charlie. It would be fun to cry. To put the day off... To overeat or sleep... But, there's nothing sad about it. You see, in other drawers I come across treasures from my other children. A picture Gaela drew me when she was four years old is in my toothbrush drawer. A photo of James' first communion is in Jay's sink drawer. We love to look for Jack peering from behind a bush in the background of that photograph. James's first grade Writer's Workshop folder is under my sink. School photos seem to ooze from drawers. Consider the treasures you've held onto throughout your children's lives. The painted handprints, the mother's day cards, the locks of hair. You know and love the comfort you receive when you happen across one of them when you weren't thinking of them.

Perhaps, you were cleaning under beds, or putting dishes away and then there it is. Artwork, a story, a poem from your child's past… and so you stop and examine it. You smile as you remember who they were at that age. Who you were at that age. What you and your child were together. Eventually, you get back to the business at hand. The memory sparker is placed back where it was. But the journey it provided….the warmth you received from it… the glow you still feel… was simply lovely.

You see I didn't lose one two year old… I've lost four. And on October 28th, as Lola turns 3, I'll lose my 5th two year old. An age and time we won't return to… a toddler that will no longer exist… as a wiser, questioning, dog hugging, "I'll pick my OWN clothes out_" three year old takes her place… The previous ages of your children are also small losses you've experienced. If your child is in kindergarten, you have lost the lap sitter, daily friend, house helper, car companion. The child themselves isn't gone forever like Charlie is, but certainly the age they were and the behaviors that came with that year won't be back. But, we quietly always knew that, didn't we? And so we buried a few treasures and scrapbooked the pictures to comfort us at the times of mourning of days, ages, and youth gone by.

Don't waste time on grieving yesterday, but clearly see the child of today and join me in considering plans for tomorrow. One day, your son will be too big for you to carry to bed… or your daughter will outgrow her stroller… or not ask you to lift her up to see something… or stop asking you to put him on your shoulders. So, don't pity my loss of little Charlie, but allow me to share who he was and what we had. Invite me to cry or reminisce…. And I'll allow you to share your child's stories of the lost days of little feet as well.

What reminders have you kept around your house of your loss or loved one? What have you discovered other people holding on to?

What items are your favorite? Stick a picture here of your loved one with some of the items you cherish today.

Grief is a Dangerous Animal

I suppose many people consider zoos as animal jails....habitats of prison. Perhaps you suspect that these animals prefer to be set free to the wild to live as they always have....

Animals in the wild lead lives of compulsion and necessity within an unforgiving social hierarchy in an environment where the supply of fear is high and the supply of food low and where territory must constantly be defended and parasites forever endured. What is the meaning of freedom in such a context? Animals in the wild are, in practice, free neither in space nor in time, nor in their personal relations. **(Life of Pi)**

This textual sketch of animal wildlife reflects my new discovery of personal freedom. Freedom is not defined by a lack of bars, but by the ability to exercise free will with one's time, space, and relations. Animals, and anyone whose survival is continually threatened, do not have this luxury. Grief can free you... a willing suspension of other's opinions. A change that forces a new life upon you. An ability to influence or choose that new life's direction. The newly and deeply bereaved are cloaked in sorrow, hastily building walls of protection. Keeping further pain away. Protecting the offspring. Pacing and anxious to sense new dangers. The deeply grieving often sustain a prolonged fight for survival, which restricts freedom and brings us down to the levels of animals... But, as healing occurs and you learn to adapt to the permanent damages that remain, freedom is possible. Break down some walls. Choose your new life. Cast away the pull towards anger, addiction, misery, and self pity. Breathe deeply. Nurture and care for another child who is desperate for care, freedom, and comfort... yourself.

Zoology and Religion. I suspect that in both of these departments, our human tendency towards self-centeredness is dangerous. In religion it leads to a lack of faith in God. In zoology, it leads to a possibly fatal misunderstanding of dangerous animals, or to a cruel treatment of an essentially innocent animal.

Animals that escape from zoos often times are found back in their zoo habitat within 48 hours. They are timid and prefer the expectations and safety the zoo provided. Imagine breaking down the door of a modern family and screaming that they are "Free_ Run to the woodlands. Live in the jungles_" Picture yourself running into a local workplace and throwing copy paper in the air and overturning tables... "Run_ Get out_ You're free_", you yell. Naturally, we embrace and prefer the entrappings of modern life and the patterns that rule our lives.

The zoo animal differs from his brother in the wild. He has no enemy. No shortage of food. Outstanding veterinary and health care. A local and clean water source. We have made him a modern home such as our own. Invite a homeless man to have free medical and dental care, meal service, and a fresh shower and sink. I don't think he'll complain. It's simply our lovely personification of animals that have us shunning zoos... our emotions filter our understanding of their existence.

I certainly don't attempt to defend zoos... I KNOW society doesn't see much merit in them and perhaps would even like to see them eliminated all together. Yet, I also know religion is viewed in much the same way in the modern age... and both conceptions seem to hold a concern for one's freedom... an impression that freedom is compromised or lacking for the parties that find themselves inhabitants of either... zoos or religion.

Charlie escaped me. He openly loved me. I whole heartedly loved him back...and then he was gone. And so I race to God.

You see I love Charlie and God is love. It's logical that I would look for him there. You are no less free in your religion than you are in your love.

Death lashes you with searing wounds. If you are new into the journey, you may suspect that my pain has been easier or lighter than your own. That your own freedom from pain won't be possible. That you lack the strength or support to follow my steps. You might enjoy thinking I couldn't possibly have hurt as deeply as you do and speak with such lightness. Stop now. Make a cautionary note for your mirror... "Symptoms of self pity are appearing".

I lost my 2 ½ year old son without warning and without final good byes. I screamed and collapsed into shock. I experienced momentary blindness when I spotted a patch of the pool's blue out the kitchen window. I stumbled with hands out calling to my older son...helpless, terrified. I spent 21 hours out of 24 awake, at his bedside for 6 days... I actually suspect and fear deeply that my little buddy Charlie was deceased for that entire week. I seem to remember blocking out a small voice inside. I was afraid to let my husband know. I feared it was a lack of faith and kept that fear from my prayers... But, when I'd crawl onto Charlie's hospital bed and pray or speak directly into his mouth, there was a different smell. Not bad, just empty. Something was wrong. When I'd hold his eyelids and try to get a pupil retraction with a flashlight, it didn't look like him. His eyes were dark and unmoving. When I'd place my hand on his forehead in prayer or pleading a slight brown liquid would drip from the corner of his mouth... I'd wipe it away quickly, desperately... My husband would hurt if he saw it... The doctors may suddenly stop all efforts... I kept it inside... and smoothed his cheek lovingly. I left him behind when the week was over. His car seat, rather than his smile, was there in my review mirror. I returned to 4 children who were broken from first hand trauma, loss, and experiences.

I extend these deeply private experiences, to offer hope to the deeply hurt and grieving. Walk in our footsteps from the early days. Survival is possible.

Grief and loss will provide you with multiple escape routes. Self pity, addiction, anger, and misery are readily available. But remember that the story of the life you lead after you've lost will always start with your loved ones name. Don't allow them to be the reason for awful outcomes in your life. Take your time. Go slowly. Live quietly. And then you'll hear it…. Deep inside. The way out of the pain. Follow and live in the love…and God is love.

Today you must love. Love yourself. Smile. And then love the day.

Out Town is a Family

Yesterday when Gaela posted that sentiment I smiled. It is indeed. Her facebook remark was referring to the support of Charlie's Turkey Trot. Soccer coach Matt Dacey had asked that his son's school be added to the registration and she posted her appreciation for all of the schools. Coach had been a silent member of Team Charlie until he recently wrote to us about a scare of his own... a loved one's life at risk; who gratefully survived. He mentioned his more profound appreciation for children, family, and life from his experience... and sharing ours.

Coach Dacey nominated Gaela for a national soccer award for inspiring others. He pledged his support, Virginia Rush soccer's support, and even that of his little son Willie's school (Montessori Children's school) of her Turkey Trot. Willie had loved the Captain Awesome story of Jack's this summer and had become attached to the stories Dad shared of Jack.

Yesterday, as Gaela left for league soccer training, she made a plan to see Coach Dacey and bring him a race poster for his son's school. As she drove towards the fields of Red Millelementary, she heard sirens... Coach called and said not to come. Stay away. There had been a bad accident... but, Gaela was already in thecrawl of traffic and upon it. A fireman waved her into Red Mill's parking lot... She nodded in recognition; he had been to our home once... he had tried to save Charlie. The firetruck blocked off the parking lot after she entered. Gaela jumped out anxiously to confirm it wasn't a family member..or Coach. It wasn't. It was a young girl who had been struck by a car.... and the Nightingale helicopter slowly descended in front of her. She watched for a long time, but thehelicopter didn't leave. She couldn't see Coach... and she finally drove backwards until she could exit over a curb.

Coach Dacey had been visiting with a parent minutes before practice was to begin... A bag of hand me down clothes for his son. A quick hello. And then- A father's yell... Coach looked up and saw the car, the girl, his young player struck. A young vibrant Rush soccer player that was training that evening... an anguished father. Stunned friends.

We thank you for supporting her opportunity in this award. We ask that you pray first, though, for this young child. Her father. Her family. We ask that you pray now. Pray. Now. I have never felt the power of prayer in my life as during our battle with Charlie. Pray. Now.

By Lauren King   The Virginian-Pilot

© October 6, 2011

VIRGINIA BEACH

An 8-year-old girl was flown to Sentara Norfolk General Hospital with life-threatening injuries after she was struck by a car in the 1800 block of Sandbridge Road on Wednesday.

_About 5:45 p.m., the girl had arrived with her father at Red Mill Elementary School for soccer practice, said Master Police Officer Adam Bernstein, a police spokesman. While her father was getting a second child out of their vehicle, the 8-year-old girl began to cross the street on her own.

The father told police he yelled at her to stop. She paused, appeared to look both ways and then crossed. Witnesses on the other side of the street told police they were also yelling at the girl to stop, but she stepped into the path of a car traveling west on Sandbridge Road.

At 8:30, Bernstein said the girl had been stabilized at the hospital, but her injuries were still considered life-threatening.

This article is dated, October 6th, Jack's birthday. We begged little Charlie to send this young spirit back to her parents if she was trying to join him. We prayed and asked often for prayers for this young child over the next few weeks. She was a stranger to our family but, she reminded us of so many personal horrors. We feared we would witness the loss of an entire family through her tragedy.

In late November, I received a call from the young girl's mother. Megan Berotti, her daughter, after over 50 days in the hospital would be discharged on November 23rd, and join us the next morning, November 24th, to celebrate Charlie's Turkey Trot. This was a memorial 5k and a celebration in his memory that we had visualized on the morning he died.

Perhaps you doubt the power of prayer.

We never doubt the kindness and cool of Charlie. That is so him.

The Beginning of Our End

Grief is the sense of loss. Mourning is the action of loss. Our grief may accompany us for some time to come but, we are slowly packing up the mourning. Charlie does not deserve to be the reason for any prolonged sorrow in lives that he only gifted with sunshine and silly nonsense. We've entered new lives. I often said they were lives we never wanted. Today, I consider simply them lives we didn't seek. But, we are seeking_out fulfillment and excitement in our new normal... or as we call it- "Because of Charlie...".One day when we are asked about how we- became... or did... or decided to.. or started to... or realized that... One day, we will smile and begin our story... I had a son... I had a brother... And because of Charlie...

As we remove the bandages of mourning, we marvel at the healing that has begun... The early battles of grief engaged us completely.. And now, in our 5th month, I pause to record our emotional history. The highlights and lessons that brought us relief... A final record of our most profound discoveries......

NOW I know....

I never wrote to be understood. I wrote to understand.

My maintenance of this internal conversation was like constant counseling... considerations, reflections, evaluations, and grief scrambled from the keyboard all over the screen. Like emptying out a toy chest or messy garage, it often helps to pull everything out and then consider what you have... Decide what's worth keeping and rid yourself of the garbage. Self pity was one of the first things I outgrew.

In days of grief, consider maintaining a personal, private journal....

But, NOW I know...

Today, in your days of joy you should maintain a journal for your children...

Open a computer document and share your thoughts of them, you, and your lives together... If you read emails daily you have time to share yourself permanently with them. If only a few thoughts a day.

NOW I know...

I wrote publicly because death will come to us all. Prior to Charlie, death only happened to other people... I certainly didn't consider the day he would come to us. And when he did, we found that for us, well... It is and was as bad as you always wondered.

And yet, we have discovered the most amazing things about ourselves, each other, and life.

NOW I know.

To Grieve is Human...

Because of Charlie I have discovered that grief is universal. It is felt by people around the world and throughout time and through a variety of losses... Consider one of my early musings...

"Some of you are hollow just like me, aren't you? I knew it the minute you entered… You lost your son, your little girl, or maybe you just hurt… So you are here, too. But, you're standing on the fringes and curious... hiding a bit, aren't you? You wonder if my loss could really be as bad as yours.. Isn't that a strange thing that satisfies us? The hollow people? How large the badge of pain?"

Now consider the reflections of poet Emily Dickinson I uncovered this past week written over 150 years ago....

I measure every Grief I meet With narrow, probing, eyes – I wonder if It weighs like Mine – Or has an Easier size.

It's no coincidence.

Those who have lost... death's survivors, are instantly connected. To meet another is to know another. To know another is to understand. To be understood by another in your depths of loss is a place of safety.

If you have recently fallen into grief through the loss of a loved one, please know there are others ahead of you who have also been down.

They have left footprints. Follow them... Follow me as I follow them. It is always sound practice as you begin travels to a land you've never been, to inquire of those who are on the road out.

Grief may join us throughout our lives but, mourning doesn't fit us very well anymore. So we begin to pack it away. And as we walk towards our finish line, I'll share more of what we have seen and how we have changed as we were seeking peace, searching hearts, and chasing Charlie.

Please put a sticky note on this page and hand it to a friend who lost somebody. Then leave them alone.

You have just lost somebody you love very much.

You will survive. Keep reading. This will be a very hard road... a life you never wanted. You may not have the motivation to go forward...but, you will because you must. Roll your eyes...but keep reading. I know where you are... I've been there. These are things I wish I had known...I'll keep it simple, because you are quick to cry and take offense...and don't want to listen and you're a mess. You really are. Told you I've been there.

First, you will be hollow....with splashes of horror. Float through this. Do anything you'd like. Don't worry about doing things because you think you HAVE to... There are no expectations. A mental snow day. Stay cozy. Stay quiet. Think. You will move out of the hollow people soon enough.

You may be thinking:

* This is strangely normal at times...

* You may think early on... Ok, it's over. That wasn't so bad. It's not... Shock brings early pains in waves.

*What am I supposed to do?

* What is this all about?

* Is this real?

* What now? What ever?

* Maybe I'll have another baby, adopt, be a foster parent, get remarried, start dating... You will be desperate to fill the hole the loss left.... There is no piece that fits.. Its funny to think about though... We even joked about advertising we wanted to babysit boy girl twins...or even just the boy. As James, said, "We would've hated them all."

This must be like waking from a 20 year coma.... You certainly remember a lot, but hasn't everything just changed in an instant?

And who KNEW how many questions you need answers for... church service, tombstones, prayer cards, memorial cards, announcements, obituaries, funeral homes, what items of clothes they will need. No shoes, the feet won't show....

Who KNEW?! Was it a child? Did they give you the final heartbeat page? Or a hair clipping? Or handprints? Did you know some funeral homes sell jewelry of the loved ones thumb prints pressed in gold? We passed on the "Thumbsies"... It is a head shaking-what the hell kinda time, isn't it?

Just so you know:

* nights are harder than days...don't drink caffeine or take stimulants...rest when you can

* you will have moments of sadness or horror... or moments of normal...

* You won't be able to make many or any decisions... It's so weird, isn't it? Your mind is protecting you. It's blocking thoughts.

My children and I couldn't pack the day after the funeral for a trip. We had NO IDEA what was going on or what we needed...James and I laughed at how few pairs of shorts he brought and how many, many shirts. Before that I had bought Charlie cute comfortable clothes for his wake- I wanted to see him look comfortable; his last days were so uncomfortable looking with the wires and machines. "So comfortable clothes for my final memories!", I thought...After that I went on to buy a nice shirt and tie like his brothers for him to wear... I just assumed he would be walking in that funeral home with them or wrestling them on the lawn. Denial. I still have that shirt and tie and see it everyday. Its not a reminder of him. It's a reminder of me. "Poor thing", I think of those days... and "Attagirl" for how far I've come.

It happened over and over again like that. Your silly jello mind...It is soooo soft, isn't it? It's ok to laugh. This is the craziest world a human can enter. And no one else knows you are there. It's as if you had fun house mirror contact lens in your eyes. The world and people certainly change so much and yet, it is impossible to explain what you see or how confused you feel. Remember, your family members may have the same vision and others have also seen what you've seen. Its nice to be understood... Reach out or read others thoughts. It will comfort you. Talk to your family or spouse... or take this book to bed with a pen and talk to me.

But, guess what?! Please know- your partner or family members may NOT want to talk about it. You will feel offended. Really? Tighten up. It's easy to get mad at them for not being more help to you. You're angry anyway so misdirecting it towards them is just the flip of a switch. Easy. But, think about it...what if you like silence in a movie theater and your spouse wants to comment on each scene? Would that drive you crazy? Should he really be offended? Would there be a solution?

If one spouse needs to talk to heal and one needs thinking instead, then go find your answer elsewhere. Talk to someone else... write it down... Go to free meetings... Remember, some people understand and master math by listening to the teacher and some must work the problems out themselves. Who cares? This means nothing. Two adjoining puzzle pieces should have a lot in common when you look at them. But, it is their differences that will make the puzzle pieces fit and belong to each other. So it goes in marriage... If grief shows you some differences, learn with curiosity...and then find a solution. Holding one responsible for their response to a death is like holding them responsible for their hair color. It is who they are... The safer they feel in their response, the faster they will heal.

The waves are washing in and out with reality. Wait--I feel ok.. Is it over? Far from it. And then its back. Grief is a treadmill. Having never been exposed to grief, your exposure tolerance will be very low in the beginning. A quick thought. A flash of their face... or last moments. You'll cry. Or get angry... or write... or shake your head...or talk about it... But, YOU'LL do something with it. Always do something with it. You handle it your way. You are in control. Not grief.

Then, when the moments gone, you'll be walking and moving again. Perfect. Our family calls it "dosing up". You handle as much as you can- in the beginning it will be very little- and then you put it away. Put it away. In the beginning days of the hollow people your tolerance to the truth will be very low... and crying at the reality is the most common way to handle it.

You must not ignore, push away, or get so busy that you never see or feel any emotions...because you will not heal... Time may close things up for you... but the emotions will be in there still. You never let them out. So one day, you will be fighting very hard to keep them in through medications, narcotics, or alcohol, perhaps.... Or they will come out at inappropriate times... like when a secretary makes a mistake... or your grandchild spills a drink... You'll find yourself in instant rage... and wonder how you got there...

That is why we care. That is why we love and nurture ourselves and want to heal and want to thrive. We look at our surviving loved ones and do not want to make them suffer the loss of another- if even they simply lose the person you used to be for them. You will also realize in time that you want to survive, thrive, love, and live because of your loved one... Rather than clinging to the pain like a measurement of your love... you'll realize I want an excellent life because this entire last part of my life story will always begin with my loved ones name. You will not want them to become the involuntary reason for terrible things to exist or happen. There is no love in that... Love is tough, isn't it?

Any bright side to this horror of the hollow people?

YES! You should, can, and will do the best if you do WHATEVER you feel like doing.... WHATEVER. Nice, right? Pancakes for dinner? Sure....No dinner? No problem. Sit on the porch at 4 am? Yep. Shot of tequila with a friend? Ok. You will want quiet. You will not want to be social. You will not want to talk very much.... But— twinkies? Have at it!

YES! You will have so many offers of help in the beginning...take it all.

YES! Your body and mind are defending you, and helping you. There is a natural course you need to follow... listen to your heart (what u feel like doing)... not your mind... (What should I do?) Your mind is a fluffy mess.

YES! Who YOU were before the loss is still there.

My husband and I laugh a lot. We really find the smallest things funny. That continued after our loss...perhaps slow at times, but it was always us. I remember my husband and I were prepared and waiting for the doctors in the consolation room. We knew our son Charlie was gone. We wanted to handle the "there's no chance" speech our way. We had fought, prayed, researched, and exhausted every option and we understood our situation. We did not need any silly grief counselors and were prepared to tell them that. But seconds before the doctors entered the room... we stared at each others tired faces, took a deep breath, and then.. Started laughing hysterically. At some point the photo id badge of Jay was on my shirt and mine was on his. We had worn these for 6 days and simply do not understand how or when they got switched. We just lost it through laughter in mid-tired-exhale....

James, Gaela, and I remember sitting politely visiting with a very young grief counselor during that week. She had read our story from the file and was speaking as if we were all lifelong best friends..."Don't you all hate how small those lockers are at school! Are they still like that, Jim?", she asks smiling at James. I could see the annoyance on their faces. And then we hear a toilet flush, a door open, and Jack wanders in for the first time... She smiles at him and says, "You must be Charlie's twin." Jack just smiled awkwardly, probably thinking, "Where the hell's the joke?" and Gaela, James, and I could.not.stop...laughing....His confused face smiling stiffly... Her sweetly voiced strange comment... What in the world, indeed. It helped to realize we were all still in there somewhere.

Your progress can't be measured in time but, what you do with time. So don't try to get over it. Get through it. If time passes without your grief, then the pain will remain inside as the outside wounds heal. It will hurt you or others in time and may never be removed. Grief and cry and cleanse now.

It could take years before some people can even handle a holiday...Tighten up. Be hard on yourself. Have high expectations... I can do this... Keep moving forward....

I spent my first weeks desperate to find a cure for the grief...books, therapy, journals...

Guess what?! The grief is the medicine! You don't get over it...you get through it..

If someone close to you has experienced a loss...

You can say:

* I will stay with you. I won't leave you.

* I will listen when you are ready.

* I will leave you alone.

* This stinks. It is really as bad as you feel (those in grief need to feel the pain is justified)... I'm so mad... This is so unfair...

(I finally met a man in my neighborhood, who's 18 year old daughter died right before Charlie... It felt good to have him swear about how terrible it is for us while he laughed and shrugged and shared what had helped him. Yes, this is an occasion for some swearing...)

You can:

*take care of all of the necessary things for them, since they are deep inside and you can not join them. This allows them to be hollow...Their minds are injured. They should not be thinking of car pools, buying laundry detergent, etc...

* Leave a calendar of meals, babysitters, carpools, hair appointments: color coded and easy to read...think jello mind.

* Yes-Great gifts are babysitters, hot meals, gift certificates for meals, friends to come and clean/do laundry, hair appointments, massages......automatically schedule them... put on calendar. "If you ever need anything..." doesn't count. They will not ask. If you sincerely want to help, schedule it. Create one master calendar for all to use.

Www.CARECALENDAR.ORG is easy and online.

Give your friend a way to text or email a cancellation if needed... they don't need or want a conversation.

* hair appointments and massages help the person feel better and leaving the front door is the biggest step of the first stage's journey.... It shouldn't be a long time before they do so....

*Babysitting should be done at a friend's house... Those in grief need a break. Need their home. Need a chance to cry or to sleep. Having the peace of mind that a child has delightful distractions makes it easier and faster to heal.

There are not a lot of wrong things to say... A lot will be forgotten anyway. They will be most grateful for the doers. For the tasks that are done so they can sleep or mourn. For the love and fun you give their children. For the length of time you walk with them.

Do not speak to them often and then stop all together. Or tune out. They will worry they have lost you. That somehow they should have healed already. That you've lost patience with them. Keep a steady pace. There are specific things future months will need so you don't need to frenzy in the first month or so...pace it out.

If you have lost someone, what are you worried about outside of grief? Think of your obligations, finances, tasks, goals.... Anything. Now show someone you truly love the passage above and your list..

If you know someone who has lost a loved one and you would like to help, please hand them this passage and a pen. Write a note in the passage that says "Read me and then make your list. Leave on doorstep by tomorrow at noon!" Those in grief are embarrassed to ask for help. If you speak to them, they will not focus and thank you politely without comprehension. Allow them to read the passage at their own rate and to consider their worries in private. Leaving the book on the doorstep doesn't require them to entertain or explain a thing.

There ARE thanks to be given

I haven't written in a while... I look back at the two month and 4 month PC (post Charlie) me who began her entries that way– "I haven't written in a while"- I look back and I pity her. Wasn't it all so overwhelming?! Well, I haven't written but, I have been thinking of writing... Most of my thoughts nowadays are in journal form...internal conversations I use to process our progress, our current disposition, our deepened understanding of ... well, of everything. You see we started at minute one, second one, knowing nothing. Knowing nothing. We had no personal experience with or prior education in grief. I recommend you review my words or read a book or two a year on someone's experience. By doing so you will be invaluable to friends who suffer. You will be invaluable to yourself. I wish I had more preparation. We knew nothing. Not of grief's symptoms, its course of attack, weak points of entry in a person, remedies, distractions, duration, experiences and understandings per age level, expectations... the navigable routes through its rough terrain. We often say, "We just don't know." My family was surprised that I considered paying a therapist to move in with us in the beginning weeks. But, frankly, that would be a luxury similar to having a nurse in the home for newborn triplets. I wanted to simply have the best care possible for such a wide range of trauma, understanding, processing, questions, and tears.

We are so thrilled that we did partner with excellent grief counselors from the beginning who walked the walk with us. We are grateful for Father Rob Cole, our spiritual advisor, who baptized Charlie, gave him last rites, funeralized him, and planted and blessed twin trees for Charlie and Lola on their birthdays. Young, but strong tall trees, with remembrance stones in front. Trees with the promise of tree climbing branches in years to come and blossoms each year on his angel date in May. Perhaps his branches will bear the weight of little nieces and nephews one day.

As you age you begin to feel older, don't you? Eyes a bit weaker? Back hurt a bit more, perhaps? Anyone have the leg nerve flare ups? Delightful. Perhaps you remember when an affliction such as these began you bemoaned them. You were shocked, you talked about it, you sought relief, and you found yourself commenting on it to sooooo many people... and often. After a few months, you now live with this new pain or flare up... It isn't gone but, you've learned to co-exist. To adapt. Some may assume the pain has gone away. Nope... it's there, alright. You have simply learned acceptance and coping strategies.

So there you have it. The pain for us... of our loss of little Charlie is still here. It is the same. We have only conquered the shock. WHO would guess it is still here 5 months later?! We simply have learned to co-exist with it as if it were a backache. We do believe and understand the truth-Charlie is gone...and it hurts at times as greatly as the first time. I'm not sure that acceptance is what we feel. It seems in a way to suggest we permit grief's presence. No, grief is certainly not welcome. We simply understand and believe that Charlie is physically gone. We also believe and understand that he remains with us spiritually. We feel him, see his hand in things, and thank him often for sticking around. If you are a person in grief who wonders how we removed the pain so quickly, rest assured. **The pain remains.** But, we are not hindered by it as much. A man's strength builds to match the enemy he wrestles. We are extremely strong defenders. Grief and pain are no match. We laugh a lot. Grief is aghast. We talk about him a lot. Grief stops just short of entry–it can't remind US that Charlie's gone. Grief lingers outside waiting to hurt us.... Come on in, grief, we were just talking about him.... Grief slinks away. Lola asks to buy Charlie a hat and gloves.... Grief pounces on her mother's heart... how sad little twinless twin... deep exhale, perhaps? A tear? No chance!

"Sure, I say. A hat is a good idea. Which one would he like?" She proudly picks the cammo hat and says, "Charlie likes being a soldier." Its nice to continue to have a brother named, Charlie. A son named, Charlie. What a nice moment we have together. Lola places it in the Charlie Chest when we get home. She calls to the sky to tell Charlie in heaven we got him a hat. I slip a note in the hat about my morning with Charlie and Lola... in case she forgets... and somewhere, grief slinks quietly away... We are a bit too fresh faced open positioned, talky talky about this boy, our loss, our fears.... We love and listen and remind and help each other. Our tears cleanse and the breath comes easier. Grief wants us to retreat. To suffer. To sit with sad thoughts in our heads all day. Like the monasteries of old that Freud said were the hiding places of those who couldn't face or cope with life. Ha! Silly Grief- we will not hide in our monastery of misery. Grief begs us to sleep in. Sleep often. To hide the pain with addictions, distractions, medications....no chance.

DO NOT NUMB YOUR GRIEF. YOUR GRIEF IS THE CURE. THE PAIN IS THE PATH OUT. YOU WILL GET STRONGER AS NEEDED. YOU WILL LOVE YOURSELF. YOU WILL MOTHER YOURSELF. YOU WILL KNOW WHEN TO HAVE YOUR SWEATPANTS AND ICE CREAM PITY BREAKS AND WHEN TO MOVE ON...... BUT, ONLY IF YOU STAY IN IT. FOLLOW YOUR HEART IT KNOWS HOW TO GET THROUGH IT. YOUR HEAD HAS NO CLUE.. HEART-WHAT YOU FEEL ...NOT YOUR HEAD... WHAT YOU THINK.

Grief wants us to excuse poor behavior, to treat the children with fragility, to handicap them emotionally, to pity them. Why? They had a gift name Charlie. He made us so very happy. We loved him. We miss him. Why pity us? Because we loved him so much? I polled every child and Jay individually on this question.... Do you wish Lola has been a single birth so that you would not have to have experienced all of this? Of course not!, every single one said. Would you want Charlie to be born again tomorrow knowing full well that this would be the inevitable unchangeable outcome? Absolutely they all said....

BINGO!

It **IS** better to have loved and lost than never to have loved at all. And secondly, by volunteering for all of this pain to simply have the time with him again has certainly placed us firmly in camp acceptance and confidence. We KNOW we can handle this beast of grief if we are willing to have it come again. Isn't that something? Backed right into it, didn't we? And yet, there it is... BOY, OH BOY, MY BOY CHARLIE... DO WE LOVE YOU OR WHAT?! Lola and I will place a little blanket outside and read this louder to you. WE LOVE YOU. You will not be the reason for anyone of us to fail, to be yucky, to be angry... We will have heartache, new goals, laughter, and touching memories, increased humanity, stronger dedication to each moment, each dance... because of Charlie.

As Daddy says, we will probably one day have 3-4 grandsons named Charlie also. We laugh at silly daddy... The kids love that idea! We love you today and forever. Charlie, remember how we all say "I love you" to each other and the response is "I love you more...." WEELLL... stop by and listen and you'll hear.... "I char you." "I char u more." Because of you. You were the softest lip kisser, strongest neck hugger, head shaking dancer, racing to hug you front door greeter.... And because of you... We char each other even more. Thank you, sweet, sweet boy.

Thank you, God for sharing him. Your son, Charlie, is simply beautiful. He was so perfectly matched for our family puzzle. You did beautifully God... Please allow him to lead us home to him through out our lives and run to greet us when we arrive.

Please consider for a moment someone you know who has lost a loved one. Today they will think of that person privately and quietly...and often. Reach out to them and tell them you were thinking of them. Arrange for a time to meet for a quiet, gentle talk. The car ride to the coffee shop may be a bit squeezed... For now you are a bit more aware of the white elephant who's been sitting between you for so long... But, after a great and lightening conversation you may be able to remove months of age from your dear friend. Start in this way,

"I have often thought of you. Then I think and wonder.... if I'm thinking of you so much, how much you must be thinking of your son. (Or daughter, mother, husband, etc..). I wanted to hear more about your experience through all of this. You really deserve to have somebody listen and I really want to know more."

NOT only is this a great way to help a friend....this a great way to help your child if they are grieving. Plant your feet and talk about the process in a "no big deal" kind of way. You have removed the monsters. You have turned on the lights.... The child can see grief a lot more clearly and it isn't such a predator after all... It isn't the prowling beast the child may sometimes hear stepping around the outside of their hearts. Or fluttering memories that quicken the heart or blush the cheeks or send sour to the throat. Invite your child to sit side by side and eat an ice cream or throw a fishing line or walk through a mall..Side by side allows for increased comfort in a little heart... and offer a little grief talk... praise their wisdom... their maturity....their growth... If they cry, praise them.... "Ahh, there it is... a few more tablespoons of pain are all gone, dear, well done!" And then close with some orange juice or ice cream... I always say, you can't cry after orange juice....the sweet washes all of the sour out...Try it! Dare your child on a regular day to have a big sip of really good orange juice and dare them not to smile. Make a big deal.... drum roll... pour the glass annnd, the cup is up to the lips ladies and gentlemen annnd... HE Did NOT... Oh, there it is!!! He smiled, ladies and gentlemen. He smiled.

(OJ has been my tears clean up for their entire lives...)

We don't have all the answers now... We still worry about so much for our children. Their feelings... Their responses...forgetting homework– grief symptom? Falling asleep after school– is it here? Is grief back? Why is he mad or forgetful? Why are they calling each other names?

That's parenting.

Parents worry. Will she be a leftie? Why did he write the d backwards? Does that mean something? He cries a lot. Does he cry too much? Why does he tease his brother? Why did she do so badly on the test? What does this mean? That? Over there? Does that mean he'll be tall? Be mean? Be a golfer? We always look for potential pitfalls or signs to reassure us. I tell my students parents every year... "The apple doesn't fall far from the tree. Your child will do well and live a truly great life that is familiar to you. I wish I could tell you all not to worry because it is true.... **But,** your child will do well and be successful because you DO worry, evaluate, and monitor your parenting..."

You have helped me so much. You have created a community mother for my family. I am humbled... I fell so hard and felt so shattered and deeply injured when this tragedy occurred. I kept trying to get to the other children ... to Jay... but my mind was clouded. My legs were shaky. My heart was badly damaged. I could only sense their injuries were very great as well but, I had no sense of common sense. My mind seemed to throb gently like a dim shaky light bulb that only reinforces its diminished functioning.

I remember Gaela's RUSH Team Charlie ran like gazelles across the Jersey fields with memorial bands for Charlie...for Gaela. He had died the day before... He wouldn't be laid to rest for days... and they already had her running... and playing mad.. And getting satisfaction. We sat on the sidelines with a twinge of jealousy...at her opportunity for physicality and her company of friends...

Jay and I joked about running through the concession stand overturning popcorn carts and snow cones to replicate the grief busting Gaela was doing on the field. We giggled as we pictured ourselves wrapped up in the tent as we head for zee hills leaving sticky sweet chaos behind...We smiled at the wit of our dysfunctional minds... those were some weird days of weird disconnected thoughts... Weren't they?

For the children's best intentions, I opened a facebook page. More Team Charlie started to collect... One face called out encouragement and I looked at their little facebook face and cleaned the scrapes off my heart... I told them I hurt....and I missed my boy. Two dozen sweet friends shouted textual "You CAN do its".... I brushed the hair from my eyes and sat a little taller. Spoke a little calmer.... 1000 faces soon greeted Lola each morning at breakfast... She delighted in the Team Charlie bracelets, the dragonflies, the silly faces, the funny people...

Jack would read over my shoulder... "She teaches at my school", he'd say... "and so does she"... I glance up to see his eyes are still glazed but, focused on reading... his mouth moves around silent words... He smiles and turns to get some milk... still smiling.

Gaela packs for her first tournament without us. We have to remove some of the many framed pictures and Charlie toys in her bag so that she has room for her uniform. She grabs his blankie.... Team Charlie Colorado steps in... Gifts, food, sideline cheers, hotel deliveries. Her Colorado gal pals take her first post Charlie picture... We are shocked to see it. She is smiling. An honest, open smile. Jay says "How about that?" I silently rummage through a junk drawer of batteries and wires to find an old lipstick and return to stare again over his shoulder at her veritable joy reflected in the picture...My eyes water with joy, my lips shine with pomegranite passion as Jay glances up at the fruity smell. God bless you, Team Charlie Colorado... You mothered her when her mother could not. May your children have a bounty of mothers throughout their lives as well.

Soon all 50 states are on the team... Parenting magazine join the team. Mom Congress joins the team. Gaela is asked to speak on Capitol Hill this Spring at their next Congress about the "Power of Mothers".... Mothers...Of course, there is me... But, then there is Jay, the hair braiding- love to vacuum Jay-mother. And then there is you... Men and women of all ages and backgrounds who have mothered us all. Then she has herself, as she is learning the power of mothering her own needs. She will speak slowly of your maternal power, the gift of love and guidance... She will speak of course... because of Charlie.

At times we were overwhelmed. We wanted to stumble...or sit... or waste time... But there were too many people walking with us... Too tight... too close. We had to continue the walk. We are grateful for our community mother you created. Kind words as we went to bed. Gentle words that started the day. Dragonfly sightings. I simply can't wait to share with you the journal of this journey in completed fashion. We have all come so far.... You have done it. You have been the heroes in this tragedy. You have assisted in life saving the injured. In the beginning days, we would have "Charlie sightings"... we all would see him in the store or work or from the back or in a crowd.... You see desire is a dominant parent of belief and reality's vision....

You really hurt for us... You really desired us to heal. You made it happen. Now, how could we ever thank you? How could you even hold the weight of your gift to see how immense it is? You brushed off our children, put some pieces back in place, and placed hope in their hands. Jay and I marvel at their growth. They will continue to hurt. We all will. But, thank God we have one another. I can't believe how fast we came or how many of you raced along with us.... God bless each and every one of you... May God reward the pain you felt for us, the efforts you extended to His injured hearts in our family, the love, patience, and kindness you sent disguised as meals, toys, letters, and "Keep on Goings", May God reward you all with never suffering the loss of a child suddenly or prior to their own children being raised.... So may your children live long enough to raise your grandchildren and never, ever leave in sudden loss. Haven't we all just had enough?

If you are grieving, I am so so sorry. It is so hard, isn't it?

If your friend is grieving, get to them and say,

I won't leave you. You will not lose me, too. I will be with you in silence. I will make it easy for you to grieve by helping with your day to day tasks.....I will wait for you to talk. I will listen.... You will NOT go on this grief journey alone. I am with you.... You can tell me everything as we go along...... I love u.

Thank you... so sincerely... for all of you. From all of us.

More to come soon. I char you all.

This story has been a long time coming.

Everything I write is a true and valid experience.

I have no motivation for attention. I already have a hard time responding to emails, texts, and phone calls. I don't have my own facebook. I hate when my hair needs a good wash and you see the polished society gal at the end of the aisle.... No motivation for attention...

I have no motivation for profit. I am released this on the internet.

I am not making it up... There are things I am told that I just wouldn't think of... There are things I am told that I had never known. There are wonderful answers. They make sense. I promise you my own thoughts **didn't** make sense the month after he passed. This is logical. I began this experience knowing nothing. This account reveals a lot of knowledge. It didn't come from me. So, no, I didn't make it up.

I considered making up a dream with Charlie in the first three days or so in order to comfort the children– Hey! He's ok and he's with Uncle Joe...kinda thing. I remember stooping to pick up a shell in Corolla and that thought crossed my mind and I wiped it out immediately. Honesty is our family's chain.

We've been honest throughout this whole experience.

BTW– this is only the beginning of a long, long, story.... For the sake of my other kids, I'm going to balance my time with them. This will take a few entries to write down.

BTW again– this sounds like such a heavy Charles Dickens tone...If ya know us and see us you know we're gonna be laughing... I'm not typing this thing with a powered wig and a monocle... It's just such an unusual experience that I have no reason to create it. I just have the tough task of sharing it publicly because, I would like to see my son again.

Charlie is in heaven. He is with Jesus. I know because he visited me the night before Father's Day. They both did. And I won't have another visit until I write about this experience. They didn't tell me that. I just know... I knew the next morning. So why didn't I write before this? Why did I wait so long? I couldn't. So often I wanted to write this... so often I wanted him to visit again. But I just couldn't write. Today I can. There must be a reason. Today is the day someone is meant to get this message. That's how it works.

So what is the difference between a visit and a dream? A dream is the creation of desires, fears, worries, wishes.... I have dreamt of Charlie since the visit. I dreamt that I found him. He had been lost. That was a desire. I have also dreamt that he and Lola were different ages... that was a worry, a sad realization. A visit is when you know he is dead. You know the truth and you see him and can react to this new reality with him.

James has had a visit... He discovered him sleeping in a room devoted to Charlie. He knew he had passed away in the dream but, there he was.... sleeping. James called to Gaela in the dream with excitement that he had found Charlie and his shouts to Gaela woke Charlie up by accident... Charlie woke up and cried with anger at them because they had awakened him... That is the reality. Our separation will be so brief... so quick that Charlie doesn't even notice. He was simply grumpy to have had his sleep disturbed.

Jack also had a visit. In a dream he was going to get Lola to go on a family car trip. As he looked into her room he saw her playing with Charlie. Jack knew in his dream that Charlie had already left us and yet there he was. Jack called to James and James in the dream saw him also. He explained it must be just a ghost and they picked up Lola to take her to the car, ignoring Charlie. As they left the front door it closed quickly behind them hitting Charlie and then they knew. He was really there and so they picked him up for the car trip as well. In these occasions, the children knew during the event that Charlie should be dead and yet, he is present and not surprised to see them. Often in dreams as opposed to visits, Charlie is excited to see us or the activities and settings are unusual and dreamlike.

I am certain that I have had the gift of a visit from Charlie. I was granted this opportunity in order to provide more comfort and guidance to the children through our journey.

Lola and Jack have had the most annoying argument from time to time.... Jack will purposely hug me and slyly smile at Lola while he is hugging me. She will be threatened and say, "it's My Mommy!" And he'll say, "No, it's My Mommy." "It's My MOOOOOMMMY!!!" She'll wail and he'll keep it up until I have lost my patience and get angry with them both. Why would they fight over me? I'm both of theirs obviously... I love them both the same.

Lola will hear people call me different names sometimes and she'll try them out herself. Out of the blue, she'll say, "Miss Elise, can I have a cookie...." Or "Elise, I have to go potty." or "Can I go to the store with you, Mrs. Normile." I always smile and answer her without acknowledging the switch and this seems to satisfy her.

I had a visit with Charlie. He was with Jesus. I know it was Jesus because he told me He was... I only spoke to Him and heard His voice. I never saw Him. But, I truly believe He responds to all of the names people call Him. Just like I did with Lola. I am the same person regardless of how I am addressed. So is He. I really sense that He loves each one of us and loves the many ways we show our love to him. Imagine the variety of gifts children get parents on Christmas... aren't they all wonderful? Aren't we simply hurt when we aren't acknowledged or remembered? And, of course, like any parent, He gets extremely annoyed when we fight over who He belongs to...

I explain this because He is not exclusionary. He told me his name was Jesus. Jesus Christ. But, perhaps that's because that's the name I call Him. You deserve to know that He exists. And he loves you...and here is how I know.

My visit with Charlie....

When Charlie died I wanted more than anything to see him...to dream of him. I would tell the family that constantly. I just needed to see him in dreams since I couldn't in life. But, I also knew I wouldn't dream of him until I got better...Until my mind healed more. I just knew I would **not** dream of him until my mind healed more... I just knew this and I would often tell this to my family and my friends as well...

"I just want to dream of Charlie... I just wish I could dream of him.... But, I know I won't until I'm better and not so sad." I suppose that if I was to have received a dreamlike visit from him in the early days, there would be a danger that I would desire only more visits, dreams, or sleep.

Ironically, I saw the movie *Inception* when it first came out over a year ago. It was an intricate movie and left a lot of questions unanswered. One of the central questions at the movie's end was whether the main character was in reality or in a suspended dream. He had tried so hard to get back to be with his children and to see their faces again throughout the entire movie. His wife seemed to have also confused reality with dreams in her search for her desired life. Watching this movie a second time recently, I began to see where this inspiration may have come. Could the writer have lost a child? Could he have felt the desperation to have seen them again and wrought his brain for some possible path to them? It seems to reinforce that desire I felt and explain why I felt I would not experience a visit until my grief had healed further.

Wanting to see him in my dreams so badly AND knowing that I would not until I healed more DID not make me frenzy to heal.... just like writing this event. For some reason, I never attempted to get better to see him... I just floated and it just came at the right time.

The 48 hours prior to Charlie's visit, I thought of him very little... I was worried for the other children. Jay and I spent two straight days on just their happiness... Boating to dodgeball at the Baja restaurant, clamming, fishing, tubing, even renting those bikes made for 4 on the boardwalk... One for the kids... One for Jay and I (Lola in the basket!)....We walked with them, spoke to them, read with them, wrote with them, and fell asleep exhausted....

And on the second night, I saw Charlie....I had begun the healing and so I saw him... At first it was just his image... his face... and so I recall pushing mentally and saying, "No no no... I need more." And then there he was...

I immediately knew I could spend as much time with him and ask as many questions as I wanted... but just for this one night. How did I know? An immediate, silent understanding. That is the only way to explain it. You just know. I just knew and the understanding had not come from me. I could see him all night and ask any questions.   I now have a much greater understanding of the Old Testament accounts of those who were told to follow stars or move families or build arks. It was just something I knew.

 At this point, I literally sat up and went to get a pad of paper and a pen...Seriously... I recorded this as it occurred.   I even would read it out loud over and over again at different times and at the end to be sure it was correct and Jesus would agree or modify or expand on what I had written...

I wrote to share the entire experience with the children. I wrote every little detail. Everything I saw. I wanted to get as much Charlie down on that paper as I could to give the kids and Jay. I read it to them the next morning, Father's Day. They cried. They were happy. They knew it was really him. And as I read I began to understand that I hadn't just written it for them but to share. I wanted to share Charlie with my family. Jesus wanted me to share Him with you... every little word that He said... As I read and described this encounter to the children I knew I would never have another until I wrote this blog. How did I know? It is a silent immediate understanding.

My notes are messy and all over the paper. Haphazard and crazy. So I will tell the story in sentences... I will share the actual notations as well.

So, I saw Charlie and he was running to me. And I scooped him up and kissed him. He ran to me across an empty room with a door at the far end... I kissed his belly and swung him around and he kept laughing... I finally put him down and he grabbed my hand...

"Come on...come on. Come on... Mom, come on..." He kept saying this over and over as he pulled me towards the door... I knew I couldn't go with him... I knew it was heaven. So I would say...

 "Hold on. Or just a minute. Or I just wanna talk for a minute".
But, he wouldn't stop.

"Come on...come on. come on... Mom, come on..." and he would lean forward and pull my hand... Imagine, if a two year old saw a merry go round and wanted you to bring them to it...relentless. That was the experience.

I finally had to say, "Ok, Charlie, go ahead... I'll be right there." "Ok".... *"And you will be. It will be that fast.",* a voice says immediately.

Here's what I wrote...
   Asked 2. Yes! v.happy...face so smiley–big
[refers to my asking to see him for so long! big smile]

Skin so clean, fresh air, messy cut but   [refers to messy hair cut]

DUH...IT'S CHARLIE!!!

striped ls shirt   [striped long sleeve shirt]

No neck. blue,red stripes

                    [no turtleneck or collar. A,blue stripe next to neck]

D.blue swts   [Dark blue sweatpants]

Clasping hands together

Not fully. 1-2 fingers offset but touching

[I'm trying to express here that it's not some silly angelic hand clasping...it's a casual grasp of hands, touching of finger tips, in front of him... His hands aren't lined up perfectly- slightly off... I am literally staring at him and sketching him with my words as I write so that the children and Jay can have as much of this experience as possible]

Mouth smiley-slightly agape drool

-on shiny lips-

[not truly drooling, but wet, shiny lips... opposite of the dry dying lips in the hospital... remember my gratitude for Amanda's chapstick] I write:

as I ask questions a voice, must be voice of Jesus

yes, it is. I am Jesus. Jesus Christ.

Runs to me as alwayss

excited happy lift him

kiss him.... loved it

asks me

come on come on

happy, excited to show me
like always
can't say no or I can't...
Won't accept.
Finally, Ok, I'll be right there.

And you will be. It will be that fast.*

*the bold words throughout account will be what Jesus says to me.

I did not see Jesus. The only reason He spoke was because I was permitted to ask Charlie anything and, well, he is two years old. It is him. He hasn't gotten wiser and wordier. His answers would be silly to me. My questions would be difficult for him. So Jesus simply spoke the answers to the questions I brought.

During this visit, I only receive limited information. I do not know anyone who is in heaven or how long we will live or who Charlie is with. If I asked any of those it would just be silence. I knew I would not be answered.

My actual notes say:

How lng LIFE...No ansrs   Who with? Who in heaven?   Silence.

After the funeral, during our visit to Corolla I had considered creating a dream story to share with the children. That idea left my head as soon as it came. I wanted to be on their level... I had no answers for them. Had I made up a dream, though, I would have placed Jay's grandfather in the tale for proof and comfort. Perhaps a younger grandpa, healthy, and fit to give them peaceful images. I never would have imagined to say that there was no information about others in heaven. This is another reason why I know it was not my creation.

RECAP:

So Charlie was begging me....

"Come on...come on. come on... Mom, come on..." and he would lean forward and pull my hand... Imagine, if a two year old saw a merry go round and wanted you to bring them to it...relentless. That was the experience. No matter how hard you try to talk to a neighbor, the insistent child can't stop pulling and begging until you answer them.

I finally had to say, "Ok, Charlie, go ahead... I'll be right there." "Ok" he said.....

"*And you will be. It will be that fast.*", a voice says immediately

Charlie then dropped my hand and ran through a door. I then was on the outside of where Charlie had run and yet I could see him through a window. I could see nothing else but him.

It was wonderful because, I think I would expect to simply see him being happy. I think I would expect that I would be satisfied knowing he was safe and okay. Instead, though, every time Charlie would look over and see me he would run to the window. He would smile and point. He would never take his eyes off of me or stop smiling. I could entertain him, make silly noises, make him laugh.

It made me realize that I was very welcome there as well. I wasn't left out. Any of us can go. We will be happily welcomed. If this was my creation or imagination, I would have imagined Charlie simply being happy without me in order to comfort myself. I would not have realized how easily I would be welcomed.

I wrote these notes as it occurred:

> *If I looked in windows, marvelous.*
>
> *He runs, see me, pt, smile*
>
> *Nvr take eyes of me*
>
> *Nvr stop smiling. I could entertain*

So, now that he was busy I could ask more questions. I asked about Gaela and what I should do for her.

Jesus said tell to tell her,

> *"Don't waste time on sadness. It is. It is just not your turn yet. Accept Jesus as your personal savior."*

Now, I have NEVER used that phrase and I have never understood what it even means...accept Jesus as your personal savior. It always sounded so preacher or thick. It's like when a girl might talk about a friend and tell you, "I love him but, I'm not in love with him." I seem to just get lost in that statement. That's what the whole, "accept Jesus as your personal savior" seemed to do for me. Seems lofty. Fluff. I never really understood what people meant. But, He gives me a veeeerrry cool explanation of this later.

My notes as this occurred:

G?

No waste time on sadness. It is. Its just not your turn yet. Must A J P S.

I asked about James and Jack. He said they will be cool. He used that word. And that's when I seemed to doubt the whole thing. I thought, "How do I know this isn't just me...why would you say the word "cool"?" And his reply was calm and automatic. I speak any language to the audience. (Aha!) He went on to say, "They will have struggles but, they will be cool, loving."

My notes:

J & J:

Cool.... I speak (the word adapt is crossed out) any lang. to the aud

They will have struggle but they will be cool, loving

Love them more, slow

I asked how Charlie could be happy without Lola. He said,

"its too quick. He's busy, then you're here. He's busy. Then you're here."

I asked him what hell was. He said, "Haven't you already had a small taste of it? Hell is when you **know** you are dead and you know **all** of your loved are gone from you forever. But <u>**you**</u> are not dead. You have time to change things or be sure you're right so you can have them all."

Are you ready for this?!

He then went on to say, "Charles Dickens once visited me in grief and took it as an inspiration for Christmas Carol." Think about THAT! You are not dead and have time to change things. Who would know that? Not me...or even connect that story to hell...

My notes:

Hell [arrow] Haven't you gotten a small taste?

Know ur dead

Know <u>all</u> your loved ones are 4eva gone from <u>you</u>

1)you not dead

2)time to change or B sure things strat so you can have them all

Charles Dickens visited w/ me -grief- took it as inspiration Christmas Carol

My actual notes on this next part are sufficient accounts of our conversation.

But I miss him. (I say talking about Charlie)

As you should.

Well-formed, well led people (humans) capacity for love and deep bonds that if you listen you will keep. God is love.... so you miss him because you deeply loved him. When you go looking 4 him

u look to me. Many people do only logically u loved him.... love is me. In sim. fashion some don't take a long time looking in my dir   [direction]

In other words...of course you miss him. You loved him. I'm love. You lost love so you look to me. Lots of people do when they lose a loved one but, some don't look long enough for them in my direction.

Remember, I would read this to Him from time to time to make sure it was accurate. He said this verbatim. I re-read it and He continued it using the word people (I know because I underlined it). I re-read it again at the end of the visit. He agreed and said humans instead of people. I see that written later and above the word people. It's no big deal. He used them interchangeably. But, I was writing so fast that I developed my own short hand. Underlined if He repeated those words as I re-read them. Paranthesis if He used another word.

I asked:

What about Lola's age in hvn.

          [What about her age in heaven, how could she be older than him when she sees him?]

Love is not ever based on age...Consider your real loves. var. of ages.

[In other words he said, Love is never based on age. Look at all those you really love. I'm sure you'll see a variety of ages.]

I asked:

Lola future   [What about her future?]

Always be a spec. child of Gods... half of her birth is here. Auto drawing her.

[In other words, she's halfway in heaven. Half of her birth is there and he's (Charlie) automatically drawing her in or towards him]

Now, after I had shared this entire experience with the children and Jay, we were satisfied. We knew. We doubted none of this and needed no more proof.

Weeks later, though, I had a chance to read a bit on Charles Dickens. Apparently the story of *A Christmas Carol* made the entire country do more good "than any parson's confessional" one reviewer wrote. People beared their souls and reached out to one another in ways that were uncanny for the time and culture he lived.

I remember how often I wrote that grief is universal and felt by people throughout histories, ages, and genders.

In my reading recently, I read this account of Charles Dickens and knew immediately what this man felt. He and his wife had her little sister, Mary, living with them for many years and she was a dear love to them both.

God seemed to be in His Heaven, and all was right in the world, when, on the evening of Saturday, 6 May 1837, Dickens and his wife went to the St James's Theatre. They had taken Mary and had an enjoyable evening. After returning home, and wishing each other good night, Dickens heard Mary cry out in pain. He ran to her bedroom, followed by his wife. The doctor was sent for. But she was beyond help. She died the following afternoon. He describes his grief in a letter to Mrs. Hogarth:

- *_This was about 3 o'clock on the Sunday afternoon. They think her heart was diseased. It matters little to relate these details now, for the light and life of our happy circle is gone -- and such a blank created as we can never supply.*

The entire family was thunderstruck. Mary's mother was insensible for a week. Catherine and Charles were dumbfounded. To a friend he wrote a day after Mary died:

You cannot conceive the misery in which this dreadful event has plunged us. Since our marriage she has been the peace and life of our home -- the admired of all for her beauty and excellence -- I could have better spared a much nearer relation or an older friend, for she has been to us what we can never replace, and has left a blank which no one who ever knew her can have the faintest hope of seeing supplied.

He wore her ring. In writing to Mary's mother, to thank her for sending him a lock of Mary Hogarth's hair, he said:

I have never had her ring off my finger by day or night, except for an instant at a time, to wash my hands, since she died. I have never had her sweetness and excellence absent from my mind so long. I can solemnly say that, waking or sleeping, I have never lost the recollection of our hard trial and sorrow, and I feel that I never shall.... I wish you could know how I weary now for the three rooms in Furnival's Inn, and how I miss that pleasant smile and those sweet words which, bestowed upon our evening's work, in our merry banterings round the fire, were more precious to me than the applause of a whole world could be...

We often say this also... we would trade it all for Charlie....

He told Forster he dreamed of her constantly and in 1844 he recounted a dream:

- *_.... I recognized the voice.... I knew it was poor Mary's spirit. I was not at all afraid, but in great delight, so that I wept very much, and stretching out my arms to it as I called it 'Dear'..the visions are a comfort and I know they are so real.*

In 1848 he wrote "*This day eleven years, poor dear Mary died...*"

I spoke to a woman yesterday who wanted to connect a young relative of hers with Gaela. The young gal had also lost a sibling, a sister. The woman commented that yesterday, 5 years since the loss, this girl had posted on her facebook... "It's been five years. Will the pain ever end?"

Grief is universal.

During the visit, I turned to Charlie and said in a really excited voice, "Hi, there. What are you doing?" and he said "Jumping".

My journal reads: *Jumping anything like kick/soccer feels like my manipulation.*

In other words, had I made this experience up, I would have had Charlie saying "I'm kicking or kicking the ball or playing soccer". It's what he loved to do and what would have pleased the children. This was not what he said and I made note of it.

My journal notes my next question and response I received:

Lola. What about him and Lola?

No sadness....none. No thoughts.
Separation will be very brief and unnoticeable to him.
He's busy than she's there. He's busy than you're here.

This seems to make perfect sense and support the visits my children have had with Charlie in their sleep. In one visit, James discovered Charlie sleeping on the floor in a room dedicated to Charlie. Sort of like the gazebo but, on the 2nd floor of our home. He knew he had passed away and yet, there he was, sleeping. He excitedly called for Gaela and the noise startled and woke Charlie who began to cry in anger that James had woken him. He did not seem to notice that there had been any separation from James over the prior 5 months.... He was just mad about being woken.

In another sleep visit, Jack had gone to get Lola for a family car trip somewhere. As he went to her room he saw her playing with Charlie. He also was aware that Charlie had passed away and called for James. James arrived and explained that he must not be real so they called to Lola and headed downstairs. As they carried Lola out to the car the glass door closed on Charlie and hit him. He cried and then they again knew that he was really there. They helped him into the car as well. Jack recounted this the next day, remembering details as if they came from a real event.

Visits are different from dreams. Dreams are the creation of hopes, desires, fears, and or worries. In both of these experiences our children knew the truth... Charlie had passed away and yet, there he was. And he experienced no delight or surprise at being reunited with them. It's as if no time had passed. He's busy then we are there.

At this time I woke Jay up and asked if he had any questions for Charlie. It was about 4 am. He did. These were not my questions so I will keep them confidential but the answers and explanations that I received, recorded, and shared with Jay provided him great comfort and satisfaction.

I then asked two very difficult questions as my journal reflects:

Forgive me?   [Does Charlie forgive me?]

Jesus. **Ridiculous.**
He never saw any faces, or any harm,
He was struggling, struggling, than lifted out
Snuggled, kissed, purely loved, and he's been happy ever since.

[The voice did not say Jesus but I wrote it at the time to note who was speaking so I wrote it again above to be identical and accurate to my journal.]

Does he blame anyone?

Doesn't know he's dead.

Our word....

Evthg alive... more alive than ever were on earth in heaven.

[In other words, Charlie doesn't know he's dead. In fact, he's NOT dead. That's our word for it. Everything in heaven is alive... more alive than they ever were on earth.]

Jesus now finally takes time to tell me how to teach the children and share with others about what it means to "accept Jesus as your personal savior." (AJPS)

My journal wrote exactly what I was told. I read and re-read it several times aloud to be sure it was accurate. He agreed with my record. This is what I wrote:

AJPS

Like pers. atten   [like a personal attendant]

Think of word savior

What is a <u>savior</u>   [He said it slowly like this "SAVE- your]

What does this person do?   [obvious mental response I had- "He saves"]

Your personal savior   [Think of me as <u>your</u> personal savior]

Obstacles to heaven. Ch?   [What are your obstacles to heaven? Think of   them
a your obstacles to Charlie...]

<u>You know</u> them...

Write them <u>each out privately</u>....

<u>Think.</u> I'll help you think.

Now-realize...

<u>I</u> will personally save you from them.

U must trust me and live like you trust me.

That's it. Beautifully simple and easy. Think of your obstacles to heaven... your weaknesses, your faults. Jesus will help you to think of them. Write them down and consider them. Now realize He will save you from them. Just trust that He will and LIVE like you trust Him to. Easy.

I read and re-read this to Him. The above words are underlined as they were in my journal to note that He was saying these words aloud as I re-read the notes.

I then was about to ask Jesus about Lola again and then realized that was a question I could ask Charlie... A question that he would understand... And so I turned to Charlie and my journal recorded me asking:

Want to c Lola?

[Smiling. Eyes looking excited eyebrows up,

Mouth staying slightly open, drooly red lips so diff from hosp.]

Charlie clearly loved the idea.... And went on to say per my account:

And Tems and Jackee   Gella   Daddy (almost a g sound:Dajee) Mommy

Charlie had begun to list all of us. I was writing as phontetically as possible so the children would know it was him. If this had been a dream, I would never had gotten this so right. But, it was truly Charlie so I very carefully wrote each sound so that they could know it was his voice.

Jesus commented as I was writing and I recorded his observation as he said it:

You'll know it's him u: Jack Jack.

In other words, you know this is Charlie because he said Jackie and you would have said Jack Jack... I know I personally would have referred to him as Jack Jack...

I was successful. The children cried quietly the next morning when I read their names as he had said them.

My journal then notes....

> *Silence doesn't say- about others or time*
> *-silence*

In other words, if I inquired about who else was with him or when we would join him, there would only be silence. I could not ask about anything beyond Charlie and my family in relation to Charlie.

We miss him/sad/mourn   [I said We missed him...We are sad. We mourn him.]

I could say don't bother….

[Again, this seemed too casual in wording. Would Jesus say don't bother? So I wondered again- How do I know this is real and I'm not just making this up?]

Adapt to lang and audience

[He again explained, "I adapt to the language and the audience."]

He then went on to respond to my statement of missing him…

I could say don't bother…. But, you will. Those well developed in love always do…. It's your human nature.

Here I hurried to make sure the children didn't feel put off by this or sense that He was minimizing their pain.

I was afraid the children might hear "I could say don't bother, but you will… It's just your human nature." And put Jesus off as being superior or elitist…. And so I wrote,

> *Not looking down or Tssk, Tssk…Not saying it holier*
>
> *It holier than thou…*
>
> *Loving, gentle totally loving voice…*

So I was trying to describe how kindly he had spoken to me…. And then Jesus said:

> **Most sim. to style, cadence of Chris Robin speaking to Pooh.**
>
> **A.A. Milne once sought me out.**

This is how he described His voice. He volunteered this description and it was perfectly captured. I would read and re-

read this transcript at the end to be sure it was accurate and He would say again and again this description. It was such an easy to understand explanation for how loving, patient, caring, and gentle His voice was. "Most similar to the style and cadence of Christopher Robin speaking to Pooh". And then as an afterthought, "A.A. Milne once sought me out."

This is not to say that His voice sounded like Christopher Robin but, yes the style and cadence-- that is it exactly.... Gentle and patient.

After this beautiful example and the explanation of Himself as a Personal Savior, I understood why people could listen to Him for hours on end. He can explain everything so perfectly... An outstanding teacher....

I then wrote:

All and only Charlie

[I must have inquired again about others in heaven or when things would happen in our life. I wrote this to say, I could ask all about and only Charlie.]

I then asked about raising the children. I recorded:

Any behavior problem- love more...

Wryly- G is love and I don't have behav. problems.

Love more, Not give more. C. Robin.

Rules, conseq w/gentle love.

So, in short, He told me if the children have behavior problems...love them more. He made a joke (said wryly)... Love them more.   God is love and hey, I don't have any behavior problems.... (I saw his sense of humor)

He said, I don't mean GIVE them more. Love them more... Think of Christopher Robin- give them rules and consequences but, with gentle love. It made perfect sense.

I then wrote....

Y do I trust—

Begged to see Him!

Begged to... knew and told others...

I can't see or won't see until I get back to right mind/outlook

In other words... Why do I trust this is real? Because I had always begged to see Charlie. I told others this. But, I also knew and had told others that I could not see him until I got back into my right mind.... Reading this back out loud (Jesus affirmed and said, "outlook" after I said mind. ...)

I also have known that I will not have another visit until I have shared this one with others. And although no one can control their own sleep activities, I have not had one since this one on Father's Day 2011 and today is December 8, 2011....   I am so close to finishing this task of sharing it. I hope I was right in my understanding. I hope I am rewarded with another visit when this is complete....

My journal goes on to say:

No, he won't see/visit all who ask...all prayers are ind answered

I saw Ch./got answers for ind. Priv relationship as child

Nothing public
Nothing with others…
Judged by:
Ind priv relationship
Treat him like family? Love him?

In other words, not everyone will receive these visits. Prayers are answered individually. Some people have them answered in the hospital. We are not rewarded or judged for how we behave in public. Public worship and public good deeds are important examples to others. But, we receive our rewards from others as well when we do them publicly. We will be judged solely on our own individual private relationship with God. Do we love him? Do we treat Him as part of our family? I received the answers and got to see Charlie because of my private relationship I had with God as a child.

My journal than goes on to note:

In dream I'm with Charlie…. Not observing…. Him! …Heaven is for all. Immed. welcome. Not on outside.

I am stating again here that I am really with him. We are all immediately welcome. It's not just to satisfy me that Charlie is there and Charlie is okay but, to share that I can come right in also. All of us are welcome.

JC- just voice not.   Explan. in my head clearly understood at once.

I am trying to explain how I received these answers. It was just a voice, not a face or physical person. I would just immediately understand the explanations in my head. It is similar to the visions and biblical accounts of warnings, prophecies, or commands that early followers experienced. I am not a religious leader, I just got an update about my boy. I received some help in counseling his surviving siblings. It was a visit.

School vs. home

 What not imp.   How is imp

Here, I had asked, "Should I go back to teaching school or stay at home?" His reply was simple. What you do isn't important. How you do it is. I kind of liked that. It reinforced the extent of our personal freedom. He doesn't care about the minute life details. If others judge you for working, having a big family, taking a long vacation, quitting, not getting married, travelling your whole life.... If other people judge you, that is their weakness, their obstacle to heaven. What you do is not as important as how you do it. Obviously, this doesn't allow for people to murder, sin, or be reckless... For then you would be failing on the "How" you lead your life element.

You are safe with God. That is very comforting.

I continued my questions.

What about G?   [Gaela]

She knows!

She loves me.... I wish she could feel my love more and live like she did. Love her even more.

Again, I would never have thought to express this. I'm sure it didn't even make sense to me as I wrote it. Gaela and I considered the message later. I think that we realized that she is often motivated to work hard and put forth effort to delight others, impress us, or please people. She recognizes this as encouragement to live a life where she knows she is loved, approved, and safe. She has made great progress in accepting and recognizing our approval and God's love.

My visit with Charlie was drawing to a close. Ironically, it was me that ended it. He was happy. He was the same. No time had passed. He was pulling and begging and relentless about me going with him through the door but, I could not. It was not my time.

I record this as it happens:

"I love yooooooou!", Charlie says at end.

Saw him!

Lips flat way out open

Long yooooou at end of I love you...

Head tilted....

Non chalant

No big gbye

Sep will be vry brief and unnoticeable to him.

Yes! So Charlie! Yes! Yes!

I noticed that he although he was saying good bye, it was if a child was off to their 3,000[th] day of school. A mother might call from the kitchen sink, "Have fuuuuuun!" but, she sings it out casually, habitually.

Charlie said, "I love yooooou" because we always say that to each other. Perhaps 14-15 times a day we say I love you to each person in the family. It was not an emotional separation. He knew I would be right back. The irony is that Charlie in life had crying fits if I left him to go to the store, so for him to be casual about this separation, I knew he had no realization of our side of the death experience.... Of the length of absence, of the longing.

As I prepared to end the visit, Charlie went back to playing. I recorded exactly what he was doing. I was watching him live and writing as I watched. I literally wanted to capture it all as accurately as possible for the children. I had access to him and so I attempted to literally sketch these moments with my words.

I recorded this snapshot of Charlie:

Dance fast footed

Hands in front loosely

Bent at elbow

Tongue out concentrating

Arms like invisible hula hoop

Looking over at someone thru messy hair

To have them notice....

To get praise...

          Friend height.

There is not a lot of importance to these details except that I was watching and writing this simultaneously. He was simply trying to dance. His hands were as if he was hula hooping and his feet were moving quickly. I wrote this as a textual sketch for what I was seeing. The most profound or beautiful moment I captured were the two words: friend height. If I had fabricated or dreamed this event, I would have imagined him looking up at a saintly or adult figure. Heaven always seemed a bit lofty, angelic, and perhaps formal in my own mind. Yet, there was Charlie jumping around, dancing, and looking over at someone he hoped to impress. While I wasn't permitted to see the person who joined him, I did know one thing from where Charlie was looking. It was a child about his size…. "friend height". I immediately had the sense that heaven had many, many children there.

After going over all of the information and adding words and underlining others that were emphasized a second time by Jesus, I went on to record my final moments.

Not what- how

[Again, it is not what you do in life, but how you live that is most important.]

Priv. indv. Relat w/God

Run to hug him?

Love him like family?

Like a 2 year old? Adore him?

I was noting again that we will be judged on our private, individual relationship with God. Do we run to hug Him? Do we love him like family? Like a two year old? Do we adore Him? Charlie and all children show us how we are to love and adore God. Speak to Him in your own authentic words. Thank Him for the pretty weather. Tell Him your fears and worries. Live in a way that shows you trust Him and feel His love.

I went on to write:

Love you Dear sweet God!
Char love completely.

Love God just like that…. Like u love a 2yr old.

Charlie didn't dance or do certain things to let us/me know it was Charlie—

IT WAS CHARLIE!

And as the visit draws to a close… I am satisfied. I write the final moments. At some point I had a sense Mary, his mother, was there. I knew but never saw her either.

WOW! Can't believe! Just love him. TYou dear sweet Jesus, love you so much. TY Mary-

You knew didn't you? Tyou! Tyou! Charlie is the best!

I wrote with an arrow pointing to that last sentence-

They correct me from "was"

In other words, I seem to be speaking and writing what I am saying as fast as possible. I said, "Charlie was the best" and they corrected me to "Charlie is the best". Of course. He continues to live and so I say "Charlie is the best".

My final note:

They say, "Thank You" like I'm talking about <u>their</u> child.

That was a bit quieting. In other words, imagine if your parents lent you a car to drive for several years. Perhaps you forgot it was only a loan or simply began to think of it as your own. When you visit with your parents you find yourself thanking them over and over again for the great vehicle and telling them how much you love it. They thank you in such a flattered, pleased manner that you realize it is their car. It is simply stunning in its accuracy.

I realized Charlie had been lent to us. We loved him, adored him, and hurt without him but, he is with his parents now. He is happy, dancing and can't wait for me to join him.... But when I do, he will be more of a brother and I will be the one that is welcomed and cherished for the child I am.

EPILOGUE

So now I know. Dying doesn't end a life. Dying ends **in** life. But, I still hurt greatly at times. I am human. It is our nature. Perhaps, the greatest gift we can receive in life is a child of our own. An innocent, soft, little love bundle to adore and to have adore you. I was so honored and grateful to receive my five bouncing baby blessings. God told me He loved me with each sweet delivery.

The final gifts that were delivered together- a brother and sister, my Charlie and Lola, were simply extraordinary. They were rewards for us all, gifts for Gaela, James, Jack, and Jay. "Thing One and Thing Two" came as a thanks for our loving and honest relations and efforts. Each of my children had lived lives deserving of our two peas in a pod…. And we adored them.

My children certainly and deeply hurt from our loss of Charlie but, my loss and grief seems catastrophic in comparison. It affected my sleep, my vision, my memory, my security, my energy, my focus… I'm certain the children and Jay worried at times. Perhaps at times they were stunned at the tremendous burden his loss weighed on me.

I hope they know I grieve for Charlie as certainly as they do. I also carry the grief and loss of the children's innocence and their youth and sunny ignorance…. I grieve for who they were, who I was, who we were together… Those innocent people left with Charlie. We are similar to who we were… similar but older, wiser, more fearful, more thoughtful….

Yes, God is good and my faith has never waivered. But, when I stop to consider the suffering that we have weathered, the heavy hurt that we still face…Well, I feel so sorry for them. I feel so sorry for all of us.

God in your infinite wisdom and love, You have picked the most beautiful companions and compassionate spirits with whom I have walked life's journey. My truest loves indeed exist in a variety of ages.

Look, I did it, Charlie!…I love yooooou Momma

Your Page

Please visit us at www.teamcharlietoday.com

Or write to us at enormile@cox.net